Egg Rolls & Sweet Tea

Egg Rolls & Sweet Tea

Asian Inspired, Southern Style

Natalie Keng

Photographs by
Deborah Whitlaw Llewellyn

Gibbs Smith

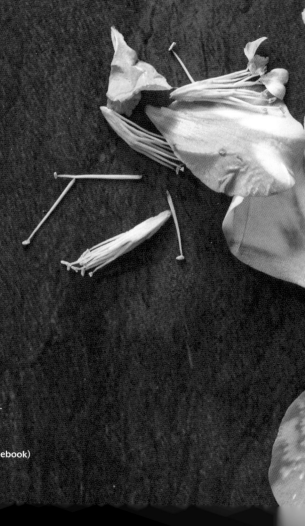

First Edition
27 26 25 24 23   5 4 3 2 1

Text © 2023 Natalie Keng
Photographs © 2023 Deborah Whitlaw Llewellyn

Published by
Gibbs Smith
P.O. Box 667
Layton, Utah 84041

1.800.835.4993 orders
www.gibbs-smith.com

Designed by Ryan Thomann and Renee Bond
Printed and bound in India

Gibbs Smith books are printed on either recycled, 100% post-consumer waste, FSC-certified papers or on paper produced from sustainable PEFC-certified forest/controlled wood source. Learn more at www.pefc.org.

Library of Congress Cataloging-in-Publication Data
Names: Keng, Natalie, author. | Llewellyn, Deborah Whitlaw, photographer.
Title: Egg rolls & sweet tea : Asian inspired, southern style / Natalie Keng ; photographs by Deborah Whitlaw Llewellyn.
LCCN 2022046924 | ISBN 9781423661498 (hardback) | ISBN 9781423661504 (ebook)
Subjects: LCSH: Cooking, American--Southern style. | Cooking, Asian. |
LCGFT: Cookbooks.
LCC TX715.2.S68 K44 2023 | DDC 641.5975--dc23/eng/20221005

To my parents, Margaret and Edward, for your undying romance and passion for life in the American South.

Contents

Introduction

CAN FOOD BE THE CATALYST FOR ACCEPTING DIVERSITY?

Can it help break down barriers and stereotypes? I've spent my adult life trying to prove that the answer is yes. This cookbook is an amalgamation of my childhood growing up in the Deep South and my experiences as I came to discover my passion for exploring the parallels and intersections of race, class, and gender through the prism of Asian and Southern family and food traditions.

Every dish tells a story, whether it's barbecue or balut. Just like putting labels on people, the judgments we make about a particular type of food or who makes it says more about ourselves than anything else. Food has always been used to bring people together and forge relationships among different cultures. What city or town in America doesn't have a sushi bar or taqueria? When we learn to love the food, we are more open to the people.

As a third daughter (considered unlucky in most traditional Asian cultures), I consider myself lucky to be born closer to Canton, Georgia, than Canton, China. My parents immigrated to Atlanta from Taiwan in the 1960s on graduate-school scholarships. When we moved into our first home, my parents found pro-segregation election campaign posters in the coat closet. As children, we were often teased and called names. Unfazed, we enjoyed the best of both worlds, attending football pep rallies and playing Pac-Man and learning math by playing mah-jongg. Navigating the social mash-up of overlaps, rejections, inclusions, clashes, and fusions, I learned grit and perseverance amidst the confusion of what it meant to be Asian, Southern, American, female, four-foot-eleven, and *strong*.

Striving to define my own principles, ideals, and "superpowers," I sought opportunity in the dissonance between cultures and values. Meanwhile, my dad's self-built home stereo system blared out his eclectic tastes in music: Andy Williams or Hank Williams? Aretha or Madonna? My teacher-mom sang along as she graded papers or whipped up a stir-fry or made plans for a weekend fishing trip while conjuring up original Asian American creations like Hot Hunan Catfish Fillets (page 140) and Five-Spice Mashed Rutabaga

Top: At five, I learned the meaning of "faith" going 60 miles per hour down a country road. "Hold on to Daddy's belt and don't let go." To him, YOLO meant embracing everything life in the South had to offer.

Bottom: Five-year-old me. "When I grow up, I want to be a brain surgeon because I'm good at cleaning fish guts."

(page 72) in her handy cast-iron skillet—perhaps not realizing how similar these tastes were to our Southern neighbors. When we ate out, however, we preferred hamburgers and barbecue. My dad loved rice porridge with a thousand-year-old egg cut up in it and fermented bean curd on the side, but in our popular mall restaurant, he also served fried chicken wings and Southern-style sweet iced tea—because *he* loved them. Between the worlds of egg rolls and sweet tea, I grew up feeling right at home.

At a moment in history when the whole world has shared an experience and endured a historic pandemic, fear-based beliefs fuel the fire of hatred. More than ever, direct experiences and interactions help engender a sense of empathy, trust, camaraderie, and a common purpose. When teaching cooking diversity classes or leading team-building tours, I share crossover Buddha-Bubba anecdotes about how we adapted to the food and culture ways of the South. And I encourage participants to do the same. From Sunday suppers to state dinners, I've seen how breaking bread—or challah, or injera, or banh mi, or egg rolls—is the sincerest olive branch, opening gateways to friendship, inspiring collaboration, and motivating people to give back. At potlucks, we "forget" that the person with whom we excitedly share our recipes might cancel our vote at the polls. We instinctively focus on good food, good health, and a sense of belonging. Who would have thought about unleashing the power of potlucks for peace?

An heirloom 1976 edition of America's most iconic cookbook, *Joy of Cooking*, includes a recipe for "a moist Oriental-style rice," accompanied by an interesting quip: "'May your rice never burn' is a Lunar New Year greeting, while 'May it never be gummy' is ours." How far we've come. In just one generation, families across North America have folded Chinese, Taiwanese, and many other Asian foods into their everyday diets. Nowadays, the advent of the gig economy and instantaneous delivery brings world cuisines to our doorstep. Online platforms enable learning and sharing, while international supermarkets and e-commerce offer a plethora of ingredients—including all kinds of rice—enticing home cooks to venture beyond their regional repertoires.

"Where are you from?" I get asked, all the time. I reply, "Georgia." "Where are you *really* from?" "Smyrna!" The theme carried throughout these pages is intended to highlight parallels and interwoven

Top: My mentor, banking executive Lissa Miller, invited me to emcee the 2018 Diversity in Action Gala awards ceremony at the Georgia Aquarium.

Bottom: Enjoyed some fresh-steamed crawdads (crawfish) when Georgia Traveler *featured my Buford Highway tours on TV.*

aspects of race, class, and gender; juxtaposed with Asian American and Southern food, culture, and traditions; and capturing the multicultural view from my family dinner table. But make no mistake: This book is also a personal collection of my favorite dishes and sauces that, I hope, home cooks will enjoy trying, tweaking, sharing, and making their own.

For centuries, mothers, grandmothers, and daughters—invisible home chefs—spent much of their lives laboring in the kitchen, making use of whatever was available (or was affordable) to fill big and little tummies, out of filial responsibility or just for survival. But rarely solely for the love of cooking. I imagine they never would have dreamed that the dishes they created would end up on social media so that the rest of us could savor and learn from their creations. I now have a profound appreciation for my heritage and the women whose flavors and umami I try to recreate.

This collection of recipes draws from my own palate and unique identity, so are they *authentic*? This is a question I am often asked, so often that I've made it a theme in this book. I would ask in return: Authentic to whom? Are popular fusion dishes authentic? If a dish has been altered to make it more palatable to an American audience, does that rob it of its culinary value? Perhaps the more relevant question is: "Does the food taste good?" So, yes, the dishes in this collection are my version of *authentic*, even if they don't fit perfectly into any textbook genre. I present these cherished recipes in the hope that they will become part of your family's supper-table favorites and evolve into your own version of *authentic*.

Will there ever be a time when food is just food? Probably not. Do we really want to be a colorblind society? I hope not. I don't want to erase the hues and flavors that make us special; I want to celebrate them. Across America, food that families like mine enjoy at home and with friends and neighbors of all walks of life reflect a myriad of influences—Native American, Caribbean, French, Spanish, and much more—converged with my multilayered heritage, from the familiarity of my hometown in Smyrna, Georgia, to the Asian diaspora that piques my interest.

DIVERSITY, AFTER ALL, IS THE INGREDIENT THAT MAKES OUR COUNTRY GREAT.

My po-po was a rebel for unbinding her feet, bucking social mores, pursuing an education, and becoming a nurse.

Wrap & Roll

My mom was an elementary school teacher for twenty-three years, and Cobb County's Teacher of the Year three times. She taught math, because she was good at it, and PE, because she delighted in playing sports with her students, who were inspired by her athletic prowess. Kids who were lucky enough to be in her homeroom, or who had PE at the same time, got to play games that applied learning principles like four square, double Dutch ("Count before you jump in when the rope reaches its apex"), and Physics Ping-Pong. Encouraging creativity in the classroom and on the field, she invented Chinese Dodgeball, a game that combined speed and angles and became so popular that our driveway turned into an ad hoc dodgeball court where students (and I) not only learned about geometry and teamwork but also, if we were lucky, got an after-school snack of sweet iced tea and rice candy, leftover pot stickers, or egg rolls.

From classroom to playground, Mrs. Keng was the consummate educator, challenging her students' sportsmanship and encouraging them not to give up when learning a new skill. One of her students went on to become an NBA player. "Do you remember me?" she asked, handing him a Georgia Tech Yellow Jackets cap to autograph. "Of course, I do! You're the only one who has ever beaten me at basketball!"

My mom's playground mantra was *practice makes perfect*. Researchers who study expertise concur: There is no such thing as instant mastery. In his book *Outliers*, author Malcolm Gladwell cited studies showing that it takes at least ten thousand hours to become a master of anything. If you've never wrapped an egg roll, expect to climb a learning curve, although it won't take anywhere near ten thousand hours. Feel free to add your own touch and be creative, and you might end up with a new hit game AND a tasty wrap-and-roll filling combination!

Just keep the faith and remember, egg rolls taste the same no matter how they look. So chop-chop. And let's get rollin'!

Top: Ever the fashionista, Mom learned to sew and used paper patterns from the Singer store to stay on trend.

Bottom: Mom was all about fashion, Dad was all about cars–and photographing his muse.

Smoked Salmon Summer Rolls

Even though transplants and visitors to Atlanta complain constantly about the Southern humidity and heat, my favorite memories as a kid are still from summertime in Georgia—from climbing rocks in backyard creeks and swimming in Lake Allatoona to walking through the dancing fountains in Centennial Olympic Park and, yes, sipping sweet iced tea on the porch. After camping out in Seward, Alaska, with a dear friend and colleague, I learned firsthand about sustainable fisheries—and got a taste of wild Alaskan salmon. I was hooked.

This recipe was inspired by my love of salmon and the hot weather of a Southern summer that calls out for cool comfort food. The smoked salmon is chilled, with refreshingly cold basil, mint, cucumber, and green onion added to the roll along with the noodles.

Makes 6 rolls

4 ounces smoked Alaskan wild salmon, chopped
½ teaspoon minced basil
½ teaspoon minced mint
1 tablespoon chopped green onion
1 tablespoon capers
5 tablespoons mayonnaise
1 teaspoon wasabi powder
1 teaspoon milk
½ English cucumber, peeled and seeded
4 ounces dried rice vermicelli noodles
6 round rice paper wrappers

In a medium bowl, mix the salmon, basil, mint, green onion, capers, mayonnaise, wasabi powder, and milk to combine. Using a peeler, create thin cucumber strips (about 4 inches long, or the width of your rolls) and set aside.

Fill a medium pot with water and bring to a boil. Cook the rice noodles according to the package instructions until al dente, about 5 minutes. Drain, reserving the hot water to soak the wrappers. Rinse the noodles with cold water until the noodles are completely cool (to prevent sticking) and set aside.

To prepare the wrappers for the rolls, pour about 1 inch of the hot noodle water in a shallow pie pan or round cake pan. If the water is too hot to touch, add in a little cold water. Submerge 1 sheet of the rice paper in the water. Working quickly, let it soak for about 15 seconds, shake off the excess water, then carefully lay the wrapper flat

continued

Smoked Salmon Summer Rolls continued

on a large clean plate or a cutting board. Let the wrapper rest for 1 minute before filling. It will feel soft, pliable, and sticky.

Place a few cucumber strips on the bottom third of the wrapper and then put about ¼ cup of noodles (a small handful) on top. Spread 1 tablespoon of the smoked salmon mixture across the top of the noodles. Fold the lower wrapper edge over the filling, close the side flaps evenly toward the middle, and roll it up until the filling is encased tightly. The wrapper is very sticky and will seal by itself on contact, so fold and roll straight— there's no rolling back! Repeat the process with the remaining ingredients. Serve immediately.

Fried Chicken Spring Rolls with Honey

When I was growing up, my family's favorite fried chicken was from the Big Chicken, a landmark KFC outpost in Marietta, Georgia, up the street from our old house. According to the local lore, it's also where a fight broke out over the last piece of fried chicken livers. This is a great way to use leftover fried chicken from those family-size buckets. Dark-meat chicken is more tender, but feel free to use whatever you have on hand. Fried chicken rolls dipped in honey definitely give you a reason to lick your fingers. Even though the chicken is deep-fried, these spring rolls are packed with vegetables and are lightly panfried using a small amount of oil. That's my rationalization for eating more of these scrumptious rolls, y'all.

Makes 12 rolls

2 small bundles (about 2 ounces) dried mung bean (glass) or cellophane noodles

2 tablespoons canola oil, divided

¼ cup thinly sliced green onions

¼ cup finely diced red bell pepper

1 garlic clove, minced

1 ½ cups grated carrot (about 1 large carrot)

12 (7-inch) square spring roll wrappers

2 cups bite-size pieces leftover fried chicken

1 large egg, beaten (or 1 tablespoon flour plus 2 teaspoons water combined for a slurry paste)

½ cup local honey, for dipping

Soak the noodles in a bowl of hot water for 15 minutes, then drain. With a large knife, slice through the stack of noodles 3 to 5 times (to prevent tangling) and set aside.

In a large nonstick skillet, heat 2 teaspoons of oil over medium heat. Add the green onions, bell pepper, and garlic and sauté 1 to 2 minutes, until fragrant. Transfer the mixture to a dish and set aside.

Using the same skillet, heat 1 teaspoon of oil over medium-high heat. Add the carrot and noodles and stir-fry. The carrot should be cooked but not soft. Remove immediately from the skillet and transfer to a large shallow dish to cool completely. (Don't skip this step—a warm filling will cause steam, resulting in soggy spring rolls.) Stir in the green onion mixture.

To assemble the egg rolls, remove 1 egg roll wrapper from the stack at a time, keeping the remaining stack covered with a clean, damp towel to prevent drying.

Lay the wrapper on a diagonal with a corner closest to you. Or, as my mother likes to say, twelve o'clock and six o'clock. Near that closest corner, spoon ¼ cup of the cooled filling mixture and a few pieces of fried chicken on top. Roll the corner up and over the filling snugly, then fold in the left and right sides toward the center to close the ends of the roll. Continue rolling the wrapper away from you. Using a finger, dab the egg or flour slurry as a "glue" to securely seal (like an envelope flap) all the edges. Set the completed roll aside, seam-side down, and repeat the process until all of the egg rolls are assembled.

Using a large nonstick skillet, heat the remaining 1 tablespoon of oil over medium heat. Add the egg rolls, taking care not to crowd the skillet. If necessary, fry in batches. As the rolls fry, use tongs or chopsticks to roll the egg rolls to allow for even frying on all sides until crispy. Transfer to a serving platter and serve honey on the side as a dip.

Chayote & Georgia White Shrimp Egg Rolls

When I was little, I would take the bus to my grandma's house after school. Nai-Nai was seventy and I was seven. She laughed at my mixed use of Chinese and English (Chenglish), and I thought she smelled like Tiger Balm. Later, Nai-Nai lived with us and shared stories of growing up very poor in the countryside of Shanxi province. To her, shrimp was a splurge, but even as she spoiled me, she still practiced frugality, using whatever ingredients were on hand. This dish combines local fresh shrimp with chayote, the marvelously crunchy Mesoamerican squash that plays a starring role in many stir-fries and adds a fresh, light cucumber-like flavor without excess liquid—which can doom crunchy spring rolls. There was no crying over spilled milk—or soggy egg rolls—at Nai-Nai's house.

Soak the noodles in a bowl of hot water for 15 minutes, then drain. With a large knife, slice through the stack of noodles 3 to 5 times (to prevent tangling) and set aside.

In a large nonstick skillet, heat 2 teaspoons of oil over medium heat. Add the green onions, bell pepper, and garlic and sauté 1 to 2 minutes, until fragrant. Add the diced shrimp and sauté until it turns pink, 2 to 3 minutes. Transfer the mixture to a dish and set aside.

Using the same skillet, heat 1 teaspoon of oil over medium-high heat. Add the chayote, carrot, and noodles and fry, stirring continuously while adding the fish sauce, salt, and white pepper to combine. After 2 minutes, mix in the shrimp mixture and continue cooking for 1 to 2 minutes more. The vegetables should be cooked but not soft. Immediately transfer the mixture to a large shallow dish to cool completely. (Don't skip this step—a warm filling will cause steam, resulting in soggy spring rolls.)

To assemble the egg rolls, remove 1 egg roll wrapper from the stack at a time, keeping the remaining stack covered with a clean, damp towel to prevent drying.

Makes 12 rolls

2 small bundles (about 2 ounces) dried mung bean (glass) or cellophane noodles

2 tablespoons canola oil, divided

¼ cup thinly sliced green onions

¼ cup finely diced red bell pepper

1 garlic clove, minced

½ pound Georgia white shrimp, peeled, deveined, and finely diced (about 1 cup)

1 chayote, peeled, pitted, and grated (about 1 ½ cups)

1 ½ cups grated carrot (about 1 large carrot)

¼ teaspoon fish sauce

1 teaspoon fine sea salt

½ teaspoon white pepper

12 (7-inch) square spring roll wrappers

1 large egg, beaten (or 1 tablespoon flour plus 2 teaspoons water combined for a slurry paste)

Homemade Sweet Chili Peach Dressing (page 161) or Homemade Teriyaki Sauce (page 165), for serving

Lay the wrapper on a diagonal (diamond) with a corner closest to you. Near that closest corner, spoon ¼ cup of the cooled filling mixture. Roll the corner up and over the filling snugly, then fold in the left and right sides toward the center to close the ends of the roll. Continue rolling the wrapper away from you. Using a finger, dab the egg or flour slurry as a "glue" to securely seal (like an envelope flap) all the edges. Set the completed roll aside, seam-side down, and repeat the process until all of the egg rolls are assembled.

Using a large nonstick skillet, heat the remaining 1 tablespoon of oil over medium heat. Add the egg rolls, taking care not to crowd the skillet. If necessary, fry in batches. As the rolls fry, use tongs or chopsticks to roll the egg rolls to allow for even frying on all sides until crispy. Transfer to a serving platter and enjoy with your choice of dipping sauce.

Note: To prepare the chayote, remove the skin using a peeler or small knife. If you have sensitive skin, oil your hands with a teaspoon of canola oil or wear food-grade gloves before peeling the chayote to prevent skin irritation. Slice the chayote in half lengthwise, then slice lengthwise again and remove the seed pit in the center. Use a box grater or food processor to grate the chayote.

Oven-Baked Country Bacon & Collard Egg Rolls

People are quirky and food trends even quirkier. Depending on where you sit or who you are, some ingredients are compost one day and gourmet the next. I love collard greens any which way, and the traditional way is to stew down a large pot of greens with ham hocks for hours until the tough greens are tender. A faster way to eat them is to chop or slice them into smaller pieces and sauté them with seasonings. My handy cleaver knife makes the task easier and allows me to enjoy this low-cost vegetable in creative, delicious ways. This recipe is a twist—or roll—on the classic pairing of pork and collards. Now that's a trend worth keeping.

Soak the noodles in a bowl of hot water for about 15 minutes, then drain. (Save the liquid to enjoy as soup broth.) With a large knife, slice through the stack of noodles 3 to 5 times (to prevent tangling) and set aside.

In a large nonstick skillet, cook the bacon 3 to 4 minutes, just until some of the fat has rendered but it is still soft. Add the green onions, bell pepper, and garlic and stir-fry for 1 to 2 minutes, until fragrant. Add the carrot, cabbage, and collards and sauté for about 2 minutes, until soft. Then add the noodles, making sure excess liquid has been drained. (Save the liquid to enjoy as soup broth). Add the salt and sauté for about 3 minutes.

Immediately transfer the mixture to a large shallow dish to cool completely. (Don't skip this step—a warm filling will cause steam, resulting in soggy spring rolls.)

Preheat the oven to 425°F. Line a large rimmed baking sheet with parchment paper or a silicone liner.

To assemble the egg rolls, remove 1 egg roll wrapper from the stack at a time, keeping the remaining stack covered with a clean, damp towel to prevent drying.

Makes 12 rolls

3 small bundles (about 3 ounces) of dried mung bean (glass) or cellophane noodles

3 slices applewood smoked bacon, diced

¼ cup thinly sliced green onions

¼ cup finely diced red bell pepper

1 garlic clove, minced

1 ½ cups grated carrot (about 1 large carrot)

½ cup thinly sliced cabbage

1 ½ cups finely chopped or thinly sliced collard greens

1 teaspoon sea salt

12 (7-inch square) egg roll wrappers

1 large egg, beaten (or 1 tablespoon flour plus 2 teaspoons water combined for a slurry paste)

1 to 2 tablespoons canola oil

Sesame Sammie Spread & Veggie Dip (page 162) or Hawaiian Mango Sauce (page 161), for serving

continued

Lay the wrapper on a diagonal (diamond) with a corner closest to you. Near that closest corner, spoon ¼ cup of the cooled filling mixture. Roll the corner up and over the filling snugly, then fold in the left and right sides toward the center to close the ends of the roll. Continue rolling the wrapper away from you. Using a finger, dab the egg or flour slurry as a "glue" to securely seal (like an envelope flap) all the edges. Set the completed roll aside, seam-side down, and repeat the process until all of the egg rolls are assembled.

Evenly place the spring rolls, seam-side down, on the prepared baking sheet. Using a pastry brush, gently brush each roll on all sides with a light coat of oil. Bake for 15 to 17 minutes, stopping to turn the rolls every 5 minutes for an even golden color. Transfer to a serving platter and enjoy with your choice of dipping sauce.

Kawaii Calamari Twice-Fried Gyoza Fritters

So *kawaii*! In Japanese, *kawaii* (rhymes with *Hawaii*) means *adorable* and *gyoza* means *dumpling*. They may be cute as dumplin's, but they disappear like hot cakes. These fritters are freshly made and double-fried crispy. For a low-fat version, boil them instead. Or gently panfry them into brown-bottom gyoza. The calamari can be any form—it will be chopped up in a food processor.

With cold tap water, rinse the water chestnuts, drain well, and finely chop. Set aside.

If the calamari is whole, cut roughly into 1-inch pieces. In a food processor, pulse-blend the crabmeat, calamari, and bacon fat for 15 to 30 seconds, until combined but a little chunky (like ground meat). Scrape the filling into a large bowl and mix in the sesame oil, salt, and white pepper.

Stir in the chopped cilantro and water chestnuts, then mix in the cornstarch.

To wrap the dumplings, put 1 teaspoon of filling in the center of 1 dumpling wrapper. Wet the edges with water and crimp the edges together tightly, by hand or using a dumpling press, to make a crescent-shaped dumpling. Make sure the wrapper is sealed with no leaks or holes.

In a frying pan, wok, or deep fryer over medium heat, heat the oil to 350°F. Fry the dumplings until they turn light brown or when they float to the surface. Transfer the partially cooked dumplings to a wire rack set over a baking sheet. Raise the heat to medium-high to increase the oil temperature to 375°F. Put the dumplings back into the oil and fry them for a second time until they turn golden brown and crispy. Serve with your choice of dipping sauce.

Makes 25 dumplings

1 (8-ounce) can water chestnuts, sliced or whole

½ pound cleaned calamari, fresh or frozen

½ pound wild-caught claw crab meat

6 tablespoons rendered bacon fat or coconut oil

1 teaspoon sesame oil

1 teaspoon salt

½ teaspoon white pepper

¼ cup chopped cilantro stems and leaves

2 tablespoons cornstarch

25 gyoza or dumpling wrappers

3 cups cooking oil

Homemade Sweet Chili Peach Dressing (page 161) or Creamy Chili Crisp Aioli (page 156), for serving

Natalie's Signature Purple Snushi Rolls

The sushi masters are undoubtedly rolling in their graves. I coined the portmanteau *snushi* as a smash-up of *snack* and *sushi*. Years ago, I invented "purple rice" by mixing black and white rice and was the first person to showcase purple rice as a healthy and eye-catching alternative to plain white sushi rolls. After my first trip outside of the United States, I realized the world was my oyster—and my rice bowl—and I was excited to explore it all. Astonishingly, there are more than 120,000 varieties of rice in the world. These rolls are fun to make, fun to eat, and pretty to serve. Unleash your creativity! And may the masters and the food critics give us grace. The sticky black rice used here (actually called "purple rice" in Mandarin) is not the same as the black medium-grain, non-glutinous heirloom rice featured in Rainbow Black Rice Salad (page 38). Appreciating what makes us similar and different in rice—or in people—may unlock magical results.

To make the snushi: Make purple sushi rice by mixing together the white sushi rice with the black glutinous rice. Cook on the stovetop or in a rice cooker according to the white sushi rice package instructions. Cover the rice and let it rest for 20 minutes. Transfer the hot rice into a hangiri bamboo bowl or a large baking dish or tray. Using a spatula or rice paddle, drizzle the rice vinegar evenly over rice. Fluff up the rice and gently fold the vinegar into the hot rice, fanning as you work to help it cool. Let the rice completely cool before using.

Put 1 sheet of nori on a bamboo rolling mat, then gently and evenly spread about ½ cup of rice on the nori, leaving ¼ inch without rice at the top edge of the sheet. Wet or oil your fingers (and cutting knife) to reduce sticking. The rice layer should be no thicker than ¼ inch. At this point, if you want a uramaki "inside-out" roll, sprinkle the rice with roasted sesame seeds, then flip the rice-covered nori sheet over.

Makes 2 rolls

FOR THE SNUSHI

¾ cup uncooked white sushi rice

¼ cup uncooked black glutinous rice (wild or sweet black Thai rice)

1 tablespoon seasoned rice vinegar

2 (7- x-8-inch) nori sheets

2 tablespoons toasted sesame seeds

⅓ cup crushed potato chips, sweet potato chips and/or beet chips

½ cup cheese curls (keep whole for filling or crushed for coating)

½ cup crushed pork rinds

¼ cup crushed honey-roasted cashews or peanuts for filling, and/or ½ cup for coating

1 avocado, sliced

½ English cucumber, sliced into strips

4 green beans, steamed

8 carrot ribbons

8 (2-inch-long) strips red bell pepper

4 asparagus, woody ends trimmed and steamed

4 pieces frozen crab sticks, defrosted

1 (5-ounce) can cooked tuna mixed with wasabi mayo

Place filling ingredients of choice horizontally (long strips work best) a couple inches from the bottom of the nori sheet. Using the bamboo mat, fold over and roll the rice and nori sheet over the fillings, gently pressing as you roll (but not so hard that your fillings squish out). Roll in the direction away from your body. For an inside-out roll where the rice is on the outside, roll the finished roll in a layer of crushed, crunchy goodness, like potato chips, cheese puffs, pork rinds, or honey-roasted cashews.

Slice into 1-inch pieces, 6 to 8 pieces per roll, and serve with pickled ginger, wasabi, naturally brewed soy sauce, or your favorite dipping sauce. Sushi rice and rolls don't refrigerate well, so make them in small batches and enjoy them fresh.

FOR SERVING
3 or 4 pickled ginger slices
½ teaspoon wasabi paste
1 teaspoon naturally
   brewed soy sauce
Dipping sauce of choice

Preppy Pink & Green Handmade Dumpling Wrappers

I love beets. So much so that I often have a leftover pot full of beet juice and don't want to waste it. I make borscht. I drink beet-carrot juice. What else? Pink dumplings!

These adorable dumplings, in two trendy hues from the 2000s, fuchsia rose and Y2K green that leverage flavorful "discards," such as the richly colored liquid that's left after cooking fresh beets or leafy greens. This dish is always a winner at my tennis team's potlucks (and matches my tennis skirt). Remember that the natural colorings are derived from vegetables, so the tones may vary or seem muted after steaming. Preppy is as preppy looks . . . and cooks!

Pink or Green Dumpling Dough

To prepare the flour, you will need 2 mixing bowls: medium and large. Using a fine-mesh strainer, sift the flour into the medium mixing bowl (after sifting, the volume of the flour will become slightly more than ¾ cup). Measure out ¾ cup of the sifted flour and transfer it to the large mixing bowl. Mix in the salt. Reserve the remaining flour for dusting. Using your fingers, push the flour outward to create a crater in the middle. Set aside.

In a microwave-safe glass, heat the beet water or green veggie juice on high for 10 seconds. Repeat in 10-second intervals until hot to the touch, about 190°F. Set aside.

Pour the olive oil into the flour crater. Working quickly, pour the hot beet water over the oil and mix with a fork for about 20 seconds, then transition to hand kneading. Use your fingers to work the dough into a ball, then press the ball against the side of the mixing bowl to pick up residual crumbs. When the dough becomes a ball, transfer it to a flat surface to knead. Keep the reserved flour on the side for minimal dusting. (Dumpling wrappers should not be over-dusted, so the dough will stay soft and pliable when wrapping.) Knead the dough for 3 to 4 minutes. Avoid adding more

Makes about 12 wrappers

¾ **cup all-purpose flour**

¼ **teaspoon salt**

5 **tablespoons plain (not pickled) beet water or Homemade Green Vegetable Juice (page 34)**

¼ **teaspoon olive oil**

1 **batch Drunken Ginger All-Purpose Asian-y Minced Pork Filling (page 135)**

Daikon Radish Dipping Sauce (page 152), Homemade Soy-Ginger Sauce (page 164), or Hot Hot Hunan Fresh Chile Sambal (page 159), for serving

continued

hot liquid or flour until the dough has been kneaded for a few minutes. If the dough is too dry or too wet, add more liquid or flour 1 teaspoon at a time. The end result should be clean hands and a dough ball that is even-colored, smooth, elastic, and supple.

Wrap the dough ball in plastic wrap and set aside to rest and soften for 50 minutes. (Actually, anywhere from 45 minutes to a whole hour is good, but 50 is said as "five tens" in Mandarin and it helps me remember how many tablespoons to use for the vegetable juice.)

To cook and eat the dumplings immediately, prepare a steamer. Line a bamboo steamer with a food-grade paper liner or moist cheesecloth, or spray with oil to prevent sticking. (If I have a napa or regular cabbage on hand, I'll remove a few outer leaves and use them as a liner. Slightly bruised leaves are fine. It's practical, eco-friendly, and pretty for serving.) Place the steaming rack or tray over at least 2 inches of water and bring the water to a boil.

Using a chopstick (or pastry cutter), divide the dough in half. Roll each half into a snake-shaped strip about 1 inch in diameter. Using the chopstick horizontally, cut each dough strip into 6 equal pieces about 1 inch big. Using your hands, roll each piece into a ball. Working in small batches of 3 to 5 at a time (to prevent the dough from drying out), press each ball into a 2-inch disc. Lightly dust the front and back of the disc with flour.

Using a rolling pin (I prefer a basic, straight wooden rolling pin without handles), roll over the entire disc back and forth once, up and down. Turn 180 degrees and repeat. Using one hand, simultaneously rotate the disc and roll the pin evenly over the edges to form a larger round wrapper, 3 to 4 inches in diameter. Dust lightly with flour if the dough sticks to the pin (but be sure not to over-flour). The center of the finished wrapper should be slightly thicker than the edges to hold the filling without tearing. Set aside and cover with a dry towel. Start filling and making the dumplings after you have a handful of wrappers ready.

To wrap the dumplings, put the wrapper on a flat surface or in the palm of a hand and put 1 to 2 teaspoons of the pork filling in the center of the wrapper. The amount of filling depends on the size of your wrapper—and your skill. If you're a beginner, less filling is easier to wrap and avoids leakage.

Fold 1 side of the wrapper over gently to form a semi-circle. Use your fingertips to crimp and seal each side of the wrapper toward the center of the dumpling. Fold and pleat in an even pattern to make a crescent-shaped dumpling that sits up. As Grandma said, "Sleeping dumplings are unlucky!" Make sure the wrapper is sealed with no leaks or holes. Leaky dumplings are unlucky, too, and they may fall apart during cooking. Place the finished dumplings on a lightly dusted flat surface.

Place the dumplings ½ inch apart in the steaming tray and cover. If your water is boiling already, turn the heat to medium (or the level where steam is coming out) and cook the dumplings for 15 to 20 minutes. The exact time may vary depending on the thickness of your wrapper and size of your dumpling. (With a meat filling, I recommend cutting open a dumpling after 15 minutes to check that the meat is cooked through and no longer pink or sticky.)

Serve hot (in the decorative bamboo steamer on a large plate) with your choice of dipping sauces. Mom likes to keep it simple with a touch of classic naturally brewed soy sauce and aged black vinegar. Pair it with a pitcher of Peachy-Plum Wine Sangria (page 198) or a local beer and you've got a dim sum home party! Remember to BYO-RP (bring your own rolling pin) and get ready to wrap and roll!

If you don't want to steam the dumplings right away, put the uncooked dumplings on a tray, cover with plastic wrap, and freeze. Then transfer the frozen dumplings to a freezer bag for storage. To cook, steam frozen dumplings for about 30 minutes, until the filling is hot and the meat is cooked through and no long pink.

continued

Homemade Green Vegetable Juice

In a blender, combine the chopped leaves, oil, and salt. Pour in the water. On the low setting, pulverize the mixture until soupy. Scrape down the sides. Blend on medium-high until pureed, stopping after a few seconds to scrape down the sides again. Strain the puree through a fine-mesh strainer into a glass measuring cup (I some-times use a lightweight saucepan, because the handle facilitates pouring). About 1 tablespoon of vegetable paste will remain in the strainer. It can be discarded or added to the filling.

1 cup finely chopped green leafy vegetables (such as bok choy or spinach)
¼ teaspoon olive oil
¼ teaspoon salt
½ cup water

Wild About Rice

Rice is life and sustenance for millions around the world. The Mandarin word for *food* is *fan*, which translates directly as *rice*. Though 112 countries grow rice, 95 percent of the world's rice is grown and consumed in Asia. Citing the ancient proverb "Behind every grain of rice is a drop of sweat," parents throughout Asia make their kids eat every grain of rice in their bowl—with one exception. On Lunar New Year's Eve, every person at the table should leave one bite of rice in their bowl, to signify abundance by having leftovers.

This section includes some of my all-time favorite dishes growing up, sticking as much as possible to my mother's organic renditions of dishes, which had her signature style (spontaneous and carefree) all over them. My grandparents lived with us as long as I can remember, so their values became our values, many of them around food and cooking. The fuss over not cleaning my plate or trying a new food was more traumatic than not cleaning my room. Much of what we ate—from glutinous black rice to strange-looking and -smelling congee toppings—were either fermented, dried, cured, or preserved.

One of my most requested cooking classes and the topic with the most questions is about rice—different rice varieties, how to cook it, how to not overcook it, how to not undercook it, why it's too sticky (less desirable when making fried rice), why it's not sticky enough (more desirable when making sushi or similar rolls). Like many wok-based, high-heat dishes, the work for making fried rice is on the front end. To avoid soggy rice syndrome, follow these simple rules: Do all your chopping first; have your oil, sauces, and seasonings ready; and strengthen your forearms and be nimble! Once the wok or skillet is hot, the cooking happens in a flash!

Rainbow Black Rice Salad

The new green . . . is black rice! From Asia to Africa, there are endless varieties of rice grown and consumed in different dishes for sustenance, traditional rituals, and cross-cultural foodways. This confetti-like salad, featuring bright vegetables inlaid with grains of deep purple, is as bold and beautiful as a visual presentation as it is a natural symphony of nutrition. Nutty and chewy without being sticky, black rice is carving a name for itself as the perfect addition to myriad salad genres around the world. The key to this salad is that you're adding the hot rice to the dressing, which is like marinating the rice in the dressing before folding in a kaleidoscope of fruit-and-veggie gems.

To make the dressing: Using a large bowl, whisk together the orange juice, lemon juice, honey, soy sauce, sesame oil, ginger, and garlic to combine; set aside.

To make the salad: In a rice steamer or on the stovetop, cook the rice according to the package instructions.

While the rice cooks, pour about 1 inch of water into a standard steamer basket in a pan with a tight-fitting lid. Spread the squash cubes in the basket, cover the pan, and bring the water to a boil. Turn the heat down to medium-low so the water bubbles steadily. Steam the squash for 10 to 12 minutes, until fork-tender (but not mushy).

Transfer the hot rice to the bowl of dressing and mix until well coated. Then add in the edamame, red and green bell peppers, snow peas, green onions, pineapple chunks, pomegranate seeds (if using), mint, half the of the cashews, and 1 tablespoon of sesame seeds. Gently combine everything together until evenly coated with the dressing.

Season with salt, black pepper, and red pepper flakes to taste. Garnish with the remaining 1 tablespoon of sesame seeds and ¼ cup of cashews and serve warm or chilled.

Serves 4 to 6

FOR THE DRESSING

¾ cup orange juice

2 tablespoons lemon juice

2 tablespoons honey

3 tablespoons naturally brewed soy sauce

1 tablespoon sesame oil

2 tablespoons olive oil

1 tablespoon grated ginger

1 to 2 garlic cloves, minced

FOR THE SALAD

2 cups short-grain black rice (not sweet rice)

1 pound butternut, kabocha, or a local variety hard squash, peeled, seeded, and chopped into ½-inch cubes

½ cup shelled and cooked edamame

½ cup diced red bell pepper

½ cup diced green bell pepper

½ cup thinly sliced snow peas

2 green onions, chopped

½ cup diced pineapple chunks

3 ½ ounces pomegranate seeds (optional)

2 tablespoons chopped mint

½ cup toasted cashews, divided

2 tablespoons roasted sesame seeds, divided

Salt

Freshly ground black pepper

Red pepper flakes

Pineapple & Chicken Fried Rice

On a hiking trip, I visited the Hostel in the Forest in Brunswick, Georgia, and stayed at one of their tree houses. I cooked with some folks at our collective dinners—a highlight of my experience—and this dish was a great way to use leftover takeout rice (or Base Camp White Rice with Quinoa, page 41), along with the pineapple we had on hand. The taste was sweet and savory, and using fruit expanded my perception of what traditional fried rice could be. For best results, refrigerate or freeze the plain cooked rice before making the fried rice. Good fried rice requires prechilled rice, so don't throw those leftovers away.

In a small bowl, combine the ketchup, soy sauce, salt, and white pepper. Mix the chicken in the marinade and set aside.

Preheat a wok over medium heat for 1 minute. Heat the oil and add the ginger and garlic. Stir-fry for about 15 seconds, until fragrant. Add the marinated chicken and stir-fry about 2 minutes, until the chicken is cooked and golden brown on the edges. Add the pineapple chunks, vegetables, and onion. Turn up the heat to high. Stir and toss for another 3 minutes. Reduce the heat to medium. Add the rice and continue stir-frying for 1 to 2 minutes, until the rice is heated through.

Serve in a bowl, and top with the pork chops, if using (or any other extra protein of choice).

Serves 2

2 tablespoons ketchup

1 tablespoon naturally brewed soy sauce

½ teaspoon salt

¼ teaspoon white pepper

1 boneless, skinless chicken breast, cut into ½-inch pieces

3 tablespoons olive oil or coconut oil

1 teaspoon minced or grated ginger

2 garlic cloves, minced

1 (8-ounce) can pineapple chunks, drained

1½ cups frozen mixed vegetables, such as peas, carrots, and corn, thawed and drained

¼ cup finely chopped red onion

3 cups cooked rice, chilled

Grandma's Teriyaki Pork Chops (page 131), optional

Base Camp White Rice with Quinoa

A simple bowl of hot, steamed white rice might seem boring, but after a long hike or bike ride and finally resting the feet around the campfire at base camp, it can be simply blissful. Using a fragrant long-grain rice like jasmine (or basmati) with a sprinkle of red quinoa, a plant indigenous to the Andean region near Bolivia and Peru, turns this basic, go-to, goes-with-everything steamed rice into comfort gourmet. Jasmine is known to be fluffier and more tender, while basmati is firmer and a tad chewier. Heads up—don't be surprised if children (ages 3 to 103) like it plain, with fried eggs, or drizzled with ketchup. As my childhood BFF used to say, it's good every which-a-ways.

If you ever find yourself in the valleys beyond Machu Picchu and want a unique way to take in the Incan heartland, take a quinoa tour and kayak through Huaypo Lake. It's just northwest of a major base camp at Cusco, where quinoa is a protein-rich superfood on every hiker's menu. However, few knew that quinoa was almost wiped out as a consequence of war. In the sixteenth century, following the conquest of Peru, the conquistadores banned the cultivation of quinoa. But defiant farmers in the Andes kept on growing it—so for Peruvians, quinoa represents freedom. That's why the quinoa tour is on my bucket list, and hence the name "Base Camp."

Serves 4

1 cup uncooked white jasmine rice

1 ½ tablespoons extra virgin olive oil

1 teaspoon red, brown, or purple quinoa

1 ¾ cups water

Using a fine-mesh strainer, rinse the rice until the draining water is mostly clear. Alternatively, to conserve water, set the mesh strainer containing the rice in a bowl of water that completely submerges the rice, and allow the rice to soak for 10 minutes, then drain and give a quick final rinse.

continued

In a medium pot over medium-high heat, combine the rinsed rice, oil, quinoa, and water and bring to a boil. Cover the pot with a tight-fitting lid, then immediately turn the heat down to a low simmer and continue cooking for 15 to 20 minutes.

Remove from the heat and allow the rice to sit, covered, for 5 minutes longer. Fluff the rice with a rice paddle or fork to redistribute the quinoa that has risen to the top.

Note: For easy meal prep, rice freezes beautifully and can be steamed to reheat, or made into Pineapple & Chicken Fried Rice (page 40) or Meal-in-a-Bowl Kimchi Veggie Fried Rice (page 48). Keep the rice frozen until ready to cook.

Beyond Fried Rice with Free-Range Eggs

I went through a period after college when I became a vegetarian and was exposed to a lot of people's cultural traditions and culinary backgrounds. I learned about plant-based patties, and I now use Beyond Burger in much of my fried rice, even though I'm no longer a strict vegetarian. It's delicious, and it has the added bonuses of being sustainable, healthy, and a good meat equivalent.

Preheat a wok for 1 minute over medium heat. Put in the avocado oil, green onions, garlic, and salt. Stir-fry for about 15 seconds, until fragrant. Add the plant-based meat and stir-fry about 2 minutes, until browned. Add the rice, then stir and toss until well blended and heated through.

Crack the eggs into a bowl, add the sesame oil, and beat well. Hollow a center in the rice and pour the eggs in the middle. Using chopsticks, scramble the eggs inside the hollow until partially cooked, then stir into the rice mixture. Add the soy sauce and cilantro and stir-fry another minute. Sprinkle with black pepper to taste and garnish with more cilantro.

Serves 2 as an entrée; 4 as a side

3 tablespoons avocado oil

3 green onions, finely chopped

2 garlic cloves, minced

½ teaspoon sea salt

½ cup plant-based ground meat or meat patties, crumbled or diced

3 cups cooked brown rice, chilled

3 large free-range eggs

½ teaspoon roasted sesame oil

3 teaspoons naturally brewed soy sauce

¼ cup chopped cilantro, plus more for garnish

Freshly ground black pepper

Turmeric Steamed Brown Rice

When my dad visited me at Harvard (a rare visit to Boston!) I went out of my way to make a special meal for him, which included brown rice. I had sourced the best ingredients to make it a memorable meal. While eating it, he said, "In Taiwan, when I was a child, we used to feed this brown rice to pigs!" We both thought it was funny, and he loved the meal, so it was a win after all.

Camellia oil is an aromatic tea oil that imparts a truffle-like aroma. It is a lovely Asian variation to try instead of olive oil. Of course, extra virgin olive oil works as well, subtly accentuating the basmati rice in its own unique way.

Scrub and dry the turmeric root. If fresh, with no darkened flesh or wrinkly skin, finely grind the turmeric using a mini food processor or string grinder. If mincing by hand, slice or julienne, then gently cut into minced pieces. Because turmeric tends to stain everything (including hands) an orangeish yellow, it isn't suited to heavy bashing or hard chopping.

In a rice cooker, combine the water, rice, turmeric, camellia oil, and rice wine. Do not stir. Set the rice cooker on the "white rice" setting if soaked overnight, or on "whole-grain" setting (which allows for extra soaking time) if the soaking time was 2 hours or less.

After the indicator says "ready" or "done," let the rice rest, covered (don't peek!), for another 15 minutes to finish steaming. Use a rice spatula to gently fold until blended.

Serves 4

1 (1- to 1 ½-inch) knob turmeric root, skin on

4 cups water

2 cups brown rice, rinsed and soaked at least 30 minutes (al dente) or overnight (tender)

1 teaspoon camellia oil or extra virgin olive oil

¼ teaspoon Hong Biou Michiu quality-controlled Taiwan rice wine

Mom's Unfried Red Rice with Berries

A self-proclaimed "Orient Express" home chef when it came to good food fast, Mom came up with one-pot "unfried rice." She probably wasn't the only busy working parent to ever do one-pot rice dinners, but intriguingly I have noticed a gradual shift in my mother's tastes as the years go by. In the dishes that she and her mother, my po-po, made during my childhood, savory and piquant Hunan and Szechuan (or Sichuan) flavors featured prominently, while her favorites in recent years are distinguished by integrating healthy grains, creative ingredients, and the chunk o' butter she loves to toss in—"Because butter makes everything taste better." Bhutanese red rice gets its extra nutrients from the mineral-rich glacial waters of the Himalayas. Here's to you and cooking outside the box, Mom!

Serves 4

1 ½ cups Bhutanese red rice

3 cups water

1 teaspoon or 1 cube vegetable or chicken bouillon

½ cup raisins

¼ cup dried goji berries

¼ cup dried cranberries

⅓ cup slivered or sliced almonds or shelled sunflower seeds

1 teaspoon garlic powder

1 teaspoon white pepper

¼ teaspoon five-spice powder

1 teaspoon salt

2 tablespoons butter

In a large heavy-bottomed or nonstick saucepan, combine the rice and water with the bouillon and soak for 30 minutes.

Add the raisins, goji berries, cranberries, almonds, garlic powder, white pepper, five-spice powder, and salt and stir to combine. Some of the spices may float on top—that's okay.

Set the pan over medium-high heat and bring to a boil. Reduce the heat to low, cover, and cook for 50 minutes, or until the liquid is absorbed. Remove from the heat and let stand, covered, for 10 minutes before serving. Fluff with a fork and gently fold the butter into the hot rice until melted and the rice is evenly coated.

Note: To use a rice cooker, follow the recipe steps above, including the soaking time, and cook according to the manufacturer's instructions.

Meal-in-a-Bowl Kimchi Veggie Fried Rice

Tempeh is a healthy, plant-based protein of fermented soybeans. It has a different taste and texture from tofu, and I prefer it in a lot of stir-fries and fried rice because it holds together better and has an earthy, savory flavor. It's a meal in a bowl because it has both vegetables and protein. The kimchi and pickled vegetables add a bright, spicy, tangy note.

To make the sauce, in a medium bowl, mix together the tahini, vegetarian mushroom oyster sauce, hot sauce, and maple syrup. Set aside.

Cut the tempeh block lengthwise, then cut into thin, 2-inch-long slices. In a large skillet over medium-high heat, heat 1 tablespoon of oil. Add the tempeh slices and brown, 1 to 2 minutes on each side. Drizzle with the teriyaki sauce, then transfer the tempeh to a plate and set aside.

In the same skillet, lower the heat to medium, add the remaining 2 tablespoons of oil, and sauté the ginger, garlic, and onion for 1 minute, until the onion is softened. Add the kale, carrot, and mushrooms and stir-fry until tender, about 3 minutes.

Add the tempeh and toss briefly to combine. Turn the heat up to medium-high and add the rice, green onions, and kimchi. Fold and toss until heated through. Drizzle with more teriyaki sauce if desired and garnish with roasted sesame seeds.

Note: Instead of tempeh, you may substitute 2 (2.6-ounce) pouches of low-sodium light tuna in water, drained.

Serves 3 to 4

1 tablespoon tahini or roasted sesame oil

3 tablespoons vegetarian mushroom oyster sauce

1 tablespoon hot sauce (such as Tabasco)

1 tablespoon maple syrup

1 (8-ounce) block tempeh

3 tablespoons olive oil, divided

2 tablespoons Homemade Teriyaki Sauce (page 165)

2 teaspoons grated ginger

2 garlic cloves, minced

½ cup chopped red onion

2 cups stems removed and chopped kale

½ cup grated carrot

1 (3.5-ounce) package shimeji mushrooms, rinsed and chopped

6 cups basmati rice, cooked according to the package instructions

¼ cup chopped green onions

½ cup chopped kimchi

1 tablespoon sesame seeds, for garnish

Ham & Egg Fried Rice-A-Roni

I discovered the magic of Rice-A-Roni outdoors around the campfire. I also grab it on nights when I crave rice but don't have the time or energy to cook more dishes to go with it. Mom's idea of adding bits and pieces like ham, extra eggs, any kind of beans, and diced vegetables turned a simple camp meal into a savory skillet meal.

Serves 2 to 3 meal portions or 6 side servings

1 6.9-ounce box chicken Rice-A-Roni
1 tablespoon vegetable oil, divided
2 large eggs, beaten
Garlic salt
¼ teaspoon white pepper
2 tablespoons Homemade Soy-Ginger Sauce (page 164)
1 tablespoon sesame oil
½ cup diced cooked ham
½ cup cooked lima beans or mixed peas and carrots
¼ cup chopped green onion
Salt

Cook the Rice-A-Roni according to the package instructions.

In a small skillet over medium heat, warm 1 teaspoon of vegetable oil. Pour in the eggs and a pinch of garlic salt. Cook, without stirring, until the mixture begins to set on the bottom and around the edges. Using a spatula, gently stir to create curds until the eggs are cooked throughout, then immediately transfer the eggs to a plate. With the spatula, break the scrambled eggs into small pieces and set aside.

Heat the remaining 2 teaspoons of vegetable oil in a large skillet or wok over medium-high heat. Stir-fry the Rice-A-Roni with the white pepper, soy-ginger sauce, and sesame oil. Mix in the ham, beans, and green onions until heated through, about 2 minutes (a little longer if the rice was cold). Add salt to taste. Stir in the eggs until combined. Serve hot, as a side or light meal.

Note: For a quick weeknight meal, you may simply wish to skip the step of making the soy-ginger sauce and instead buy my ready-to-use award-winning, You Saucy Thing Marinade, Stir-Fry & Braising Sauce.

Broccoli & Basmati Rice Casserole

We ate rice porridge at home, not casseroles, because Mom never baked. She used the oven to store pots and pans. I fell in love with casseroles (and Tuna Helper) on sleepovers as a kid. This recipe pairs mushrooms and rice—two of my favorite comfort foods—and I added pepper Jack cheese for a little spice. Feel free to substitute a milder cheese, such as mozzarella, Havarti, or Monterey Jack.

In a medium bowl, stir the broth, yogurt, sour cream, mustard, salt, and white pepper until smooth. Add in the cornstarch and stir to dissolve any clumps. Set aside.

In a large ovenproof skillet over medium-high heat, melt the butter. Add the mushrooms and shallots and stir-fry until browned and softened, 5 to 7 minutes. Add the sage and garlic and stir-fry another minute. Add the cooked rice and stir to combine, breaking up the clumps.

Stir the broth mixture to ensure any settled cornstarch is fully incorporated. Pour the mixture over the rice in the skillet. Add the broccoli and stir well. Cover the skillet and let steam until the broccoli is bright green and al dente, 5 to 7 minutes.

Preheat the broiler. Sprinkle the cheese on top of the whole dish. Broil for about 2 minutes to melt the cheese. Garnish with fried wonton strips and serve warm.

Serves 4 to 6

1 cup vegetable broth
½ cup plain whole-milk yogurt
2 tablespoons sour cream
1 teaspoon Dijon mustard
½ teaspoon sea salt
½ teaspoon white pepper
2 tablespoons cornstarch
   or tapioca starch
1 tablespoon butter
8 ounces oyster
   mushrooms, chopped
½ cup chopped shallots
1 teaspoon finely chopped
   fresh sage
3 garlic cloves, finely minced
3 ½ cups cooked basmati rice
3 cups bite-size broccoli florets
1 cup shredded pepper
   Jack cheese
Fried wonton strips, for garnish

Curried Coconut-Cauliflower Fried "Rice"

In addition to being low in carbs, cauliflower is nutritious and easy to cook. This curry recipe doesn't use curry powder—instead, it uses the scratch ingredients and fresh turmeric, available at most international markets, to get a fresher, richer seasoning. Using cauliflower instead of rice makes it a good post-workout protein-rich meal.

Using a large-holed grater or a food processor with a grating disc, finely chop the cauliflower. The texture should approximate rice grains (don't worry if the size isn't uniform). Set aside.

In a large pan over medium heat, melt 1 tablespoon of coconut oil. Using a spatula or chopsticks, scramble and break the eggs in small pieces until cooked. Transfer to a small bowl and set aside. Wipe out the pan with a paper towel and return it to medium heat.

Melt the remaining 1 tablespoon of coconut oil in the pan. Add the onions, celery, garlic, ginger, and turmeric. Stir-fry about 3 minutes, until softened and fragrant. Add the riced cauliflower, soy sauce, mirin, lime juice, and salt. Stir-fry about 2 minutes. Stop stirring for 30 seconds to let the cauliflower brown a bit. Mix in the chickpeas, cooked edamame, and cooked eggs. Let stand for 30 seconds, then stir-fry 2 minutes more, until the cauliflower is al dente and the chickpeas are heated through. Garnish with the nuts and serve with hot sauce to taste.

Note: For extra protein, top with grilled chicken or shrimp.

Serves 4

- 1 large head cauliflower (about 2 pounds)
- 2 tablespoons coconut oil, divided
- 2 large eggs, beaten
- ½ cup chopped green onions
- ¼ cup chopped celery stalks, leaves removed
- 3 garlic cloves, minced
- 1 tablespoon grated ginger
- ½ teaspoon grated turmeric
- 3 tablespoons naturally brewed soy sauce
- 1 tablespoon mirin
- 1 teaspoon lime juice
- ¼ teaspoon salt
- ½ cup cooked or canned chickpeas, drained and rinsed
- ½ cup steamed edamame
- 1 teaspoon roasted sesame oil
- ¼ cup roasted Georgia peanuts or roasted cashews, for garnish
- Hot sauce

Himalayan Red Rice & Beans

I was inspired by Sea Island red peas to make this dish in the spirit of the Southern Hoppin' John I grew up with, which we would eat on New Year's Day for good luck. The red rice is a variety grown in the Himalayas, with minerals from the glacial waters. Fresh ginger adds a touch of warm spice and also aids in digestion. I'm often asked how to store fresh ginger, which is hard to keep. Just put leftover ginger in a ziplock bag and freeze it for up to 3 months, until you're ready to use.

I like to use Pine Street Market andouille sausage, or Carroll's smoked link sausage (see Resource Guide, page 203), but you can use your favorite local brand. There's plenty of flavor in this dish to go meatless, too.

Serves 2

10 ounces smoked sausage

1 tablespoon vegetable oil

½ cup diced onion

⅓ cup diced red bell pepper

⅓ cup diced celery

1 teaspoon chili powder

½ tablespoon grated fresh ginger or 1 teaspoon powdered ginger

3 garlic cloves, minced

2 cups vegetable broth or water

1 (14.5-ounce) can diced fire-roasted tomatoes

1 teaspoon honey or brown sugar

1 cup Lotus Foods Red Rice or red rice of choice

1 (15-ounce) can red kidney beans, drained

¼ cup chopped green onions, for garnish

Sriracha (optional)

In a large saucepan over medium heat, cook the sausage until browned and firm, about 1 minute per side. Transfer the sausage to a plate and let cool, then cut into ¼-inch slices.

In the same pan, add the oil and sauté the onion, bell pepper, and celery for about 2 minutes, until the onion is softened. Add the chili powder, ginger, and garlic. Sauté for another 30 seconds.

Add the broth, tomatoes with their juices, and honey and stir to combine. Deglaze by scraping any browned bits from the bottom of the pan. Add the rice and beans. Stir and bring to a boil. Reduce the heat to low, cover, and cook for 45 minutes. Halfway through the cooking time, stir from the bottom, fold in the sausage, and cover again. Finish cooking the rice until tender and the water is absorbed.

Garnish with the green onions and a drizzle of hot sauce (if using) and serve.

Note: This is delicious paired with a side of Ginger-Spiced Sweet Plantains (page 70).

Last-Minute Lettuce-y Chicken Fried Rice

Generally, iceberg lettuce is not considered stir-fry material. But because lettuce is a staple in many fridges across America, moms have told me how much they appreciate having a fried rice recipe that not only includes meat and veggies, but—most important—caters to kids' taste buds. While this dish isn't likely to win any culinary awards, it does win over the hearts of parents cooking on a budget, or college kids who want a quick, healthy, tasty meal that isn't fast food or takeout. If you don't have fresh garlic and ginger, substitute ½ to 1 teaspoon each of the powdered versions. Kids of any age like it with a mix of ketchup, teriyaki sauce, or sriracha drizzled on top.

Serves 2

1 tablespoon naturally brewed soy sauce, divided

¼ teaspoon sugar

¼ teaspoon salt, plus more

½ teaspoon cornstarch

6 ounces boneless, skinless chicken breast or thigh, sliced into bite-size pieces

3 tablespoons vegetable oil, divided

1 tablespoon grated ginger

1 tablespoon minced garlic

1 large egg, beaten

3 cups cooked rice

½ teaspoon white pepper

2 cups shredded lettuce (any variety)

2 tablespoons chopped green onions

1 teaspoon roasted sesame oil (optional)

In a medium bowl, whisk together ½ tablespoon of soy sauce with the sugar, salt, and cornstarch. Add the chicken and mix well. Set aside to marinate while you prepare the vegetables.

Heat 2 tablespoons of oil in a large saucepan over medium-high heat. Stir-fry the chicken until cooked through, about 5 minutes. Transfer the chicken to a plate and set aside. Pour the remaining 1 tablespoon of oil into the same hot pan and add the ginger and garlic. Fry a few seconds, until fragrant, but do not brown. Add the egg and stir-fry for 1 minute. Add the rice and cooked chicken. Break up any clumps of rice or egg and toss together for 1 minute. Drizzle in the remaining ½ tablespoon of soy sauce, salt to taste, and the white pepper; toss to coat everything evenly. Lastly, add the lettuce and green onions and toss to combine. Drizzle with a little roasted sesame oil (if using) and serve hot.

Note: This dish can be made ahead or stored as a frozen meal. For children (or picky eaters), any spices can be omitted. You can substitute pork or beef for the chicken. Other diced vegetables such as peas, carrots, and red bell pepper can be used, but should be cooked or, if frozen, thawed and drained of excess water.

Veggie Mania & Wok the Garden

Most of the recipes in this chapter highlight farm-fresh vegetables. In the case of Mu Shu Wood Ear Burritos (page 79), the star of the show is a dried premium wood ear mushroom grown in the high-altitude mountains of Taiwan, recognizable by its distinctive black and tan coloring. Individual ingredients like wood ear or the okra in Okra & Tomato Stir-Fry (page 63) maintain their integrity and impart a unique flavor and crunch. Yet the finished dish is vastly superior in taste than its parts!

At eighteen, I stopped wearing leather shoes when I read that production practices harm the environment. To protest the negative ethical and environmental impacts of meat production, I also swore off eating meat (and wild-caught sea scallops) and declared myself a vegetarian. Confession: I was a vegetarian who craved meat. As a consolation and a distraction during those years as a carnivorous foodie turned herbivore, I got creative and got my hands dirty—literally.

As a shareholder at Brookfield Farm, a pioneering community-supported agriculture co-op, or CSA, I learned that "fair trade" and "organically grown" weren't just marketing slogans, they were the operating manual. Besides the sweetest just-picked corn and juiciest tomatoes, the barn and farm-to-table principles brought together the synergy—and resources—among community stakeholders: farm owners, student apprentices, residents, and restaurant owners. The results, in terms of labor, donations, expertise, and collaboration, yielded a great bounty and taught me the meaning of successful partnerships and sustainability.

Although I am no longer a strict vegetarian, I minimize meat in my diet by favoring stir-fries, where the addition of vegetables, tofu, and aromatics like chives and green onion can easily stretch meat by a factor of four. The classic trinity of aromatics—fresh ginger, garlic, and green onions, which my mom coined the "3 Gs," plus a fourth "G," garlic chives—add complexity to meat-and-veggie stir fries, while heightening the piquancy of vegetarian dishes.

America is like a stir-fry—or a jambalaya—where each ingredient has a cadence of its own, all coming together under a mélange of sauces, seasonings, and syncopation, creating a crescendo of flavors in a single dish. Like an exuberant symphony, a stir-fry should be tossed during the entire cooking process to harmonize properly. It's a reminder that we should be attentive to our actions and their consequences, so that we can come together as a country—without forgetting where we came from.

Top: When traveling, farmers markets are on my must-visit—and must-eat—list. Popular Portland Farmers Market is definitely worth a stroll.

Bottom: Back in the day, my vegetarianism seemed radical, but nowadays, plant-based foods have mainstream appeal (Wok the Garden presentation pictured).

Sautéed Lemon Pepper Snow Peas

As we emerged from the long cold winters of New England, the opening day of the farm season in April was a highlight each year at the CSA. Eager shareholders would head to the barn to say hello and check the chalkboard for featured items and the PYO (pick-your-own) list of the day. Early spring onions, sugar snap peas, and snow peas were a crunchy welcome change from the winter root vegetables. Even a cruciferous veggie lover like me could only eat so many cabbages, beets, and turnips!

Heat the oil in a skillet over medium heat. Sauté the garlic for 30 seconds, until fragrant but not brown. Add the snow peas, lemon juice, Italian seasoning, soy sauce, and pepper. Sauté for 1 minute. Don't overcook the peas or leave them in the hot pan. Serve hot. They are best bright green and slightly crunchy.

Serves 4

1 tablespoon olive oil

1 large garlic clove, minced

8 ounces snow peas, stemmed and strings removed

1 to 2 teaspoons lemon juice

½ teaspoon Italian seasoning blend or dried oregano

1 teaspoon light naturally brewed soy sauce or tamari

1 teaspoon freshly ground black pepper

One-Minute Stir-Fry

Have vegetable, will stir-fry. I need to eat more vegetables, but I get tired of salads. More than anything else, a stir-fry captures the quintessential spirit and technique of wok cookery. Fast, hot, healthy, and versatile, this speedy stir-fry demystifies this age-old culinary technique down to the delicious essentials for the beginner or experienced home chef: chop, season, and toss. The key is to have everything prepared in advance with a sharp cleaver, the perfect sauce, and, of course, super-fast cooking. Go to town with a medley of whatever vegetables and protein you have on hand, and you'll be ready to eat in 1 minute. Really.

Heat the oil in a skillet or wok over medium-high heat and add the ginger, garlic, and green onions. Stir-fry for 10 to 20 seconds, taking care to keep it from burning. Add the bok choy and sauce and continue to stir-fry for 1 minute.

Remove from the heat and serve hot over rice or noodles.

Serves 2

1 tablespoon vegetable oil

1 tablespoon minced fresh ginger

1 tablespoon minced fresh garlic

¼ cup sliced green onions

2 cups sliced bok choy (or your favorite vegetables, except soft greens, like lettuce, that wilt)

½ cup Homemade Soy-Ginger Sauce (page 164)

2 cups cooked rice or noodles

Sukuma Wiki in a Wok

A good friend of mine studied conservation biology in Kenya and introduced me to this dish. This African-style braised collard greens recipe is based on the very rustic dish from East Africa. In Swahili, *sukuma wiki* means to stretch the week when food or supplies are scarce. Traditionally, the hearty greens were served with ugali (corn fufu), a cornmeal mush that is a simple but filling accompaniment for stews.

I was excited to discover another classic collard greens recipe and learned that ugali is similar to grits! This recipe reminds me of Southern collard greens, except it's stir-fried and cooked for less time. Chopping the collard greens in smaller pieces makes it less tough and easier to chew. I have found that kale and chard are excellent substitutions for collards. Adding a dash of Hot Hot Hunan Fresh Chile Sambal (page 159) gives it an extra bite and brings out the vinegar overtones.

Serves 3 to 4

2 tablespoons olive oil
1 medium Vidalia onion, sliced
3 garlic cloves, minced
4 cups chopped collard greens
½ teaspoon curry powder
1 tablespoon Homemade Soy-
   Ginger Sauce (page 164)
½ teaspoon dried chili flakes
1 tablespoon balsamic vinegar
2 medium tomatoes,
   cut into wedges
Salt
Hot sauce, such as Tabasco
   or sriracha (optional)
Cooked ugali or grits, for serving

In a wok or a medium-large pan, heat the oil over medium heat. Add the onion and garlic and stir-fry for about 2 minutes, taking care not to let the garlic burn. Toss in the collards and sauté for 1 minute. Add the curry powder, soy-ginger sauce, chili flakes, and vinegar. Sauté for another 1 minute. Add the tomatoes and cook until heated through and the collards are wilted, about 10 minutes. Add salt to taste. Drizzle with hot sauce (if using).

Serve with ugali or grits.

Okra & Tomato Stir-Fry

Even though okra is enjoyed in parts of Southeast Asia and served steamed or as tempura in Japan, my parents were first introduced to the deep-fried version of okra in the South. It's hard to beat the taste of hot, freshly fried okra alongside a plate of barbecued pork and a glass of sweet iced tea!

My mother started cooking okra in stir-fries so we could enjoy it without the excess fat of fried okra and slime of the steamed version. Keeping it whole eliminates the "goo" factor, but if you prefer it sliced, a teaspoon of an acidic ingredient such as vinegar or lemon juice helps reduce the sliminess. Tomatoes are a colorful, flavorful addition to this dish, adding zing without the sodium of extra soy sauce. Toss them in gently at the end and be careful not to overcook.

Serves 2 to 4, as a side dish

1 tablespoon vegetable oil

1 tablespoon minced fresh ginger

1 tablespoon minced fresh garlic

1 tablespoon chopped green onion

½ pound fresh whole okra, washed

⅓ cup Homemade Soy-Ginger Sauce (page 164)

1 tablespoon balsamic vinegar

1 pint cherry tomatoes, each tomato sliced in half

Heat the oil in a skillet over medium-high heat. Add the ginger, garlic, and onion and stir-fry for 30 seconds. Add the okra, soy-ginger sauce, and vinegar and stir-fry 1 minute, until heated through but still crispy. Toss in the cherry tomato halves and gently stir for a few seconds before serving.

Chipotle Black Bean Chili

I've loved chili all my life. The Chomp & Stomp Chili Cook-Off and Bluegrass Festival supports local parks and green spaces in the historic and diverse Cabbagetown district of Atlanta, and I look forward to it every year. As a little girl, I wanted to become either a professional chili taster or a certified barbecue judge. I am neither, but in the years while transitioning from corporate executive to bootstrapped entrepreneur, I did enter a local chili contest with my mother. We shared a booth with not one, not two, but six different varieties of chili entries. I made four chili recipes and she made two. I smelled so strongly of garlic and peppers for a week that the neighborhood dogs wouldn't leave me alone. My mom is so competitive that she even competed against my chili entries. Everyone thought she was a hoot, and she won the People's Choice Award.

Melt the butter in a large pot over medium heat. Add the onion and sauté for 2 to 3 minutes, until softened. Add the cumin, cocoa, garlic, chipotle pepper and adobo sauce, and tomato paste. Sauté for about 2 minutes to bring out the flavor of the spices. Add in the black beans, pinto beans, tomatoes with their juices, and water. Stir a few times from the bottom up so everything is mixed.

Cover and bring to a boil over high heat. Reduce the heat to medium and take off the lid. Simmer for 15 to 20 minutes, until thickened. Check and stir periodically to prevent sticking to the bottom of the pot. Add half of the lime juice, half of the cilantro, and salt and black pepper to taste. If the chili is thicker than you like, add a little more water. For a thicker, richer version, blend 1 cup of the chili with an immersion blender or regular blender and mix it back in the pot.

Serves 8 to 10

1 tablespoon butter

1 Vidalia onion, diced

1 tablespoon ground cumin

1 tablespoon cocoa powder

4 garlic cloves, minced

1 chipotle pepper in adobo sauce, finely chopped, and 2 tablespoons adobo sauce (from the can of chipotles)

¼ cup tomato paste

3 cups cooked or canned black beans, drained and rinsed

2 cups cooked or canned pinto beans, drained and rinsed

1 (28-ounce) can fire-roasted diced tomatoes

2 ½ cups water or vegetable broth

Juice of 1 lime, divided

½ cup chopped fresh cilantro, divided

Salt

Freshly ground black pepper

1 avocado, diced in ½-inch chunks

Tortilla chips, for serving

While the chili is simmering, in a small bowl, mix the remaining lime juice and remaining ¼ cup of cilantro with the avocado. Season with salt and black pepper to taste. Serve the chili topped with the avocado mixture and tortilla chips on the side or crumbled on top.

Note: Chili is one of my favorite freezer meals, so this recipe makes a big batch. I portion it into smaller serving-size bowls before freezing so that it's an easy lunch box or weeknight meal. To defrost, run the bowl under hot water or immerse the frozen bowl in hot water for 1 minute, then pop the contents into a pot or microwave-safe bowl to reheat to the desired temperature.

Seasoned Tofu, Bok Choy & Garlic Flower Chives

This is my grandmother's dish and my mom's childhood all-time favorite. It is a signature item in the cooking classes my mom and I teach, and a special dish for home cooks—it's not typically served in restaurants. Flowered garlic chives are slightly stiffer than the ones we are familiar with, and we use the flower buds and every part except the woody ends in this recipe. This dish works with or without sausage. Mom sometimes substitutes kielbasa sausage from Winn-Dixie, which we, and all our American friends and neighbors, love.

Technically, *tofu* is "bean curd" and *dou gan* refers to a firm, pressed, seasoned form of tofu, similar to tempeh. Unlike what we know as fresh tofu, this version is a firm, preseasoned bean curd, with the liquid pressed out. It holds up well in stir-fries and for grilling.

All the work for making a stir-fry is on the front end. To avoid soggy stir-fry syndrome, follow these simple rules: 1) Do all your chopping, 2) mix your sauce, and 3) plate it and enjoy immediately. Once the wok or skillet is hot, the cooking happens in a flash!

If you don't have all the fresh sauce ingredients on hand or are tight on time, keep some Homemade Soy-Ginger Sauce (page 164) handy as an all-in-one substitute. I don't like drowning my stir-fries in thick, brown sauce, so I skip adding cornstarch to my sauce mixture. If you like to get saucy, make a sauce slurry by dissolving 1 tablespoon of cornstarch and 2 tablespoons of water in your sauce bowl before the final wok toss. It's all good!

To make the sauce, in a medium bowl, combine the soy sauce, hoisin sauce, soy-ginger sauce, sesame oil, and black pepper. Mix well, then set aside.

Serves 4

2 tablespoons naturally brewed soy sauce

2 tablespoons hoisin sauce

3 tablespoons Homemade Soy-Ginger Sauce (page 164)

1 tablespoon roasted sesame oil, plus more for serving

½ teaspoon black pepper

2 tablespoons vegetable oil

1 tablespoon minced garlic

1 tablespoon grated ginger

2 green onions, chopped, divided

5 to 6 stalks garlic flower chives, woody ends removed, keep flower buds, cut into 2-inch pieces

1 cup diagonally sliced pieces red bell pepper

2 cups diagonally sliced pieces bok choy

2 blocks smoked or savory baked tofu, cut into matchsticks

½ cup Taiwanese sausage, cooked and sliced in thin strips (optional)

Cooked rice, for serving

In a large skillet or wok, heat the vegetable oil on medium-high heat and stir-fry the garlic, ginger, half of the green onions, and the garlic chives with their flower buds for 30 seconds. Add the bell pepper and bok choy, tofu matchsticks, and sausage strips (if using) and stir-fry 1 minute more, until brightly colored and heated through. Pour the sauce mixture into the wok. Toss to coat for 30 to 60 seconds.

Remove the stir-fry from the hot wok immediately. Garnish with the remaining green onions and drizzle a little bit of sesame oil on top. Serve hot with rice.

Vindaloo-Inspired Ratatouille Ziti

Indian vindaloo is one of those traditional dishes that has crossed geopolitical borders to become a favorite around the world. For Brits and Singaporeans alike, vindaloo curries are one of the most popular dishes in curry houses. Vindaloo can be traced back to the Catholic Portuguese explorers of the fifteenth century. Similar to sushi, the vindaloo sauce base and marinade of vinegar and spices was a result of the need to preserve and ferment meat and fish on long voyages. Vindaloo ingredients typically include red chiles and tomatoes or potatoes brought in from the Americas.

I was introduced to ratatouille for the first time in college. It's a wonderful one-pot healthy meal for summer garden vegetables. The campus chefs thought so too, and they put it on the menu so frequently that I resorted to adding my own flavor twists from the spice bar as a change of pace. Fortunately, there are many flavor combinations that complement the tomato and onion base. One of my favorite things to add is vindaloo or vindaloo spices. If you have time, make and grind the spice paste from scratch. (When I was a job-searching graduate I never had that time, and Patak's spice pastes were goddess-sent shortcuts.)

The dish is versatile and can be enjoyed over rice or pasta, or with fresh naan or roti bread. If you have leftovers, add a cup of water or two and it becomes a spicy, savory vegetable soup.

In a large bowl, toss the eggplant cubes with the sea salt. Let it sit for 20 minutes, then rinse with water and drain, gently pressing out the excess water and salt.

In a large, heavy pot, heat 2 tablespoons of the oil over medium heat and sauté the onion about 4 minutes, until softened. Add the red and green bell peppers and sauté for another 2 minutes.

Serves 4

1 medium eggplant, cut into 1-inch cubes (about 2 cups)
1 tablespoon sea salt
4 tablespoons olive oil, divided
1 cup chopped red onion
1 red bell pepper, diced
1 green bell pepper, diced
4 garlic cloves, peeled and minced
3 ripe tomatoes, of choice, chopped
1 (16-ounce) can tomato puree
2 cups sliced semicircle pieces zucchini or summer squash, sliced into semicircles
½ cup red wine
1 tablespoon balsamic vinegar
1 teaspoon cumin powder
1 teaspoon Patak's Vindaloo Curry Spice Paste
1 tablespoon grated fresh ginger
1 teaspoon paprika
Salt
Freshly ground black pepper
1 (16-ounce) box ziti pasta
Naan, for serving (optional)

Add the garlic, chopped tomatoes, tomato puree, zucchini, prepared eggplant, wine, vinegar, cumin, spice paste, ginger, paprika, and salt and pepper to taste and mix together. Taste and adjust seasonings as needed.

Increase the heat to medium-high and cook for 5 to 7 minutes. Stir, reduce the heat to low, cover with a lid, and simmer for 20 minutes.

While the ratatouille is simmering, cook the pasta according to the package directions. Drain and toss with the remaining 2 tablespoons of oil. Serve a heaping ladle or two of ratatouille over a plate of pasta or with warm naan.

Ginger-Spiced Sweet Plantains

I was first introduced to plantains—the sweet and green varieties—by a Salvadoran classmate. They reminded me of the fried bananas served as dessert in Hong Kong eateries. They can be served as a savory side with anything but are especially good with Himalayan Red Rice & Beans (page 54). Add a good local honey and it becomes a sweet dessert. I personally like to pair these plantains with my favorite Atlanta craft beer.

Serves 4

1 tablespoon butter

1 tablespoon coconut oil

2 ripe yellow plantains, peeled and cut diagonally into 3-inch-long, ½-inch-thick slices

1 to 2 tablespoons honey

1 teaspoon grated fresh ginger

In a large pan over medium-high heat, melt the butter with the oil. Arrange the plantains in an even layer in the mixture. Fry until light brown and soft, about 2 minutes on each side.

In a small cup, mix the honey and ginger together. Drizzle on the hot plantains and serve.

Five-Spice Mashed Rutabaga

Rutabaga is a vegetable with a PR problem (see also: prunes). During graduate school, I learned to eat a lot of different root vegetables when I subscribed to a winter season farm box. It's good that I loved turnips, radishes, beets, cabbage, and rutabagas because the long winters lasted through April in New England.

It's amazing how naturally sweet a cooked rutabaga is.

Peel the rutabaga and cut into 1-inch chunks.

In a medium pot, combine the rutabaga and garlic and cover with water. Stir in the salt and bring to a boil. Reduce the heat to low, cover, and simmer for 25 to 30 minutes, or until fork tender. Drain the rutabaga and garlic and return them to the pot.

Add the butter, five-spice powder, white pepper, and sesame oil to the pot and stir to combine. Mash with a potato masher or use an immersion blender. Garnish with the green onion and serve warm.

Serves 4

1 medium rutabaga
   (1 to 1 ½ pounds)
2 whole garlic cloves, peeled
1 teaspoon salt
3 tablespoons butter
½ teaspoon five-spice powder
½ teaspoon ground
   white pepper
⅛ teaspoon roasted sesame oil
1 green onion, chopped,
   for garnish

Yellow & Green Panko Squash Fries

Panko is a Japanese-style breadcrumb that's easily found in any supermarket or online. I use a special Himalayan pink salt from the Salt Table in Savannah, a local, woman-owned business, but there are many good sea salts you can use. These squash fries are much like sweet potato fries, and are really good with Joy Luck BBQ Pulled Pork Bao Buns (page 132).

Serves 2

- 2 (5 to 7-inch-long) zucchini
- 2 (5 to 7-inch-long) yellow summer squash
- 2 egg whites
- 1 cup Japanese panko breadcrumbs
- 1 teaspoon dried Italian seasoning blend
- ½ teaspoon garlic powder
- ½ teaspoon white pepper
- ¼ teaspoon ginger powder
- ½ teaspoon fine-grain Himalayan pink salt
- ⅓ cup grated Parmesan cheese
- Avocado oil or olive oil spray
- Creamy Chili Crisp Aioli (page 156), for serving

Preheat the oven to 400°F. Line a baking sheet with parchment paper or aluminum foil.

Quarter the zucchini and squash lengthwise and cut into uniform sticks about 3 inches long and ½ inch thick. Transfer to a large bowl and set aside.

In a medium mixing bowl, gently beat the egg whites with a fork until slightly frothy.

Pour the egg whites over the vegetable sticks and toss to coat thoroughly.

In a small bowl, stir together the panko, Italian seasoning, garlic powder, white pepper, ginger, salt, and Parmesan.

Dip the vegetable sticks, one at a time, in the panko mixture, coating them entirely, then place each stick on the prepared baking sheet in a single layer. Mist the sticks with avocado oil spray.

Bake 20 to 25 minutes, until the sticks are crisp and browned. Serve immediately with the aioli.

Note: For a savory, peppery twist, I like dipping these fries in Homemade Soy-Ginger Sauce (page 164) mixed with a little wasabi paste.

Soy-Ginger Brussels Sprouts with Ham & Balsamic–Saigon Cinnamon Glaze

Are you a sprouts dodger or sprouts lover? I jokingly call this a "sprouts converter" recipe because many have exclaimed (after taking another bite off the plate), "I don't usually like Brussels sprouts!" Not to take away from the integrity of the real roasted Brussels revival on menus from pop-ups to steak houses, but the glaze takes these sprouts to new heights. To boot, Brussels sprouts are the coolest-looking vegetable in the garden, with green leafy bulbs on fat cruciferous stalks.

Serves 4

2 tablespoons Homemade Soy-Ginger Sauce (page 164)

1 teaspoon rice vinegar

1 tablespoon olive oil

2 tablespoons tahini or raw sesame paste

½ teaspoon paprika

¼ teaspoon garlic powder

3 cups trimmed and halved Brussels sprouts

¼ cup diced honey-baked ham

Balsamic–Saigon Cinnamon Glaze (recipe follows)

Roasted sesame seeds, for garnish

Preheat the oven to 400°F and line a baking sheet with a silicone baking mat or parchment paper.

In a large bowl, combine the soy sauce, vinegar, oil, tahini, paprika, and garlic powder. Add the Brussels sprouts and diced ham and, using a large spoon or spatula, toss together to coat the sprouts completely with the seasoning mixture.

Pour the sprouts onto the prepared baking sheet and spread evenly in a single layer. Pop the tray into the oven and set the timer for 20 minutes. After the first 15 minutes, give the sprouts a quick stir, then continue the roasting process for the final 5 minutes, or until the Brussels sprouts are browned with crispy, caramelized edges.

Transfer to a serving platter and drizzle with the glaze and a sprinkle of sesame seeds for garnish.

Note: You can make this recipe in an air fryer. Preheat the air fryer to 375°F, and prepare the Brussels sprouts the same way as for the oven method. Put the sprouts on the air fryer tray and set the timer for 11 minutes. After the first 7 minutes, remove the tray and give a gentle shake to toss and turn the sprouts, then return the tray to finish the cooking cycle.

Balsamic–Saigon Cinnamon Glaze

Saigon cinnamon is sweet and spicy and stronger than other varieties of cinnamon. It is a perfect match for bold balsamic vinegar. This sauce makes everything taste good, period.

Makes $1/4$ cup

½ cup balsamic vinegar

⅛ teaspoon ground
  Saigon cinnamon

In a small saucepan over medium heat, whisk together the vinegar and cinnamon. Bring to a gentle boil, then immediately reduce the heat to low and allow to simmer, stirring occasionally, while closely monitoring as the vinegar thickens and is reduced to half of the original amount.

The consistency will be similar to a rich syrup or honey and will coat the back of a spoon. Remove from the heat and allow to cool. It will continue to thicken a bit more.

Jackfruit & Pepper Stir-Fry

Mom showed me that fruit wasn't just for fruit salads or smoothies—she also used fruit in some of her stir-fries. Indeed, it was a natural, healthful way to add a sweet or tangy surprise in every savory bite. The spiky yellow jackfruit has a starring role in my international supermarket food tours. When in season, its distinct, imposing presence can be found in extra-large bins near the store entrance. It's often confused with the unrelated spiky, stinky durian fruit, so many folks are missing out on this fragrant, sweet, tropical giant (the largest in the breadfruit family) with hints of banana and honeydew melon. This dish is attractive served hot over rice for dinner or snugly tucked inside a tortilla wrap for lunch.

Remove excess liquid from the tofu by pressing the whole tofu block between 2 plates with a can of soup as weight on top for 10 minutes or while you prep the vegetables. Drain and pat dry the tofu with a towel. Cut the block in half lengthwise, then cut into ½-inch slices.

In a 12-inch pan, heat 1 tablespoon of oil over medium-high heat. Using a heat-proof spatula, spread the oil to coat the entire surface of the pan. Put in the tofu slices, filling the entire pan. It's okay to have the edges of the tofu touching one another. Drizzle 1 tablespoon of the soy sauce and 2 tablespoons of the soy-ginger sauce over the tofu and brown over medium heat, flipping once, for 3 to 4 minutes per side.

While the tofu is panfrying, in a separate medium pan over medium-high heat, heat the remaining 1 tablespoon of oil and quickly sauté the red and green bell peppers for 2 to 3 minutes. Add the jackfruit, mushroom, and ¼ cup of the green onions with the remaining 1 tablespoon of soy sauce and the remaining 1 tablespoon of soy-ginger. Gently fold in the cooked tofu to combine, then transfer to a serving platter.

Drizzle with the teriyaki sauce and garnish with the remaining ¼ cup of green onions. Serve over rice or in a wrap.

Serves 4

1 (14-ounce) package firm tofu

2 tablespoons canola oil, divided

2 tablespoons soy sauce, divided

3 tablespoons Homemade Soy-Ginger Sauce (page 164), divided

1 cup julienned red bell pepper

1 cup julienned green bell pepper

½ (20-ounce) can ripe jackfruit, drained, rinsed, and sliced (about 1 cup)

1 small piece dried wood ear mushroom, rehydrated and julienned

½ cup thin diagonally sliced green onions, divided

⅓ cup Homemade Teriyaki Sauce (page 165)

3 to 4 cups cooked rice or whole wheat tortilla wraps, for serving

Sake-Shiitake Mushroom Bake

My grandfather made homemade rice-wine moonshine in our base-ment when I was growing up. I loved a traditional country breakfast porridge of oatmeal, eggs, and a splash of my grandfather's rice wine cooked in, but I once drank a little extra left on the counter and missed the bus for school!

This is an unstuffed mushroom dish with all the tasty results of stuffed mushrooms but less work. Almost any type of fleshy mushrooms will work beautifully in this easy, layered side dish. I often use locally grown shiitake and oyster mushrooms from Ellijay Mushrooms (see Resource Guide, page 203). If you don't have sake, the best substitute is the same amount of a dry white wine—sake is a bit stronger, but the taste is similar. The creative herb-salt blends from Beautiful Briny Sea are perfect for this recipe, or you can use your favorite sea salt.

Serves 4

1 ½ pounds fresh shiitake mushrooms, cut into bite-size pieces, divided

3 cups soft breadcrumbs, divided

1 teaspoon sea salt, divided

1 teaspoon white pepper, divided

½ cup melted butter, melted, divided

½ cup sake

Preheat the oven to 325°F.

In the bottom of a 2-quart baking dish, spread out one-third of the mushrooms. Cover with 1 cup of the breadcrumbs, and lightly sprinkle with ½ teaspoon of salt and ½ teaspoon of white pepper. Drizzle with one-third of the butter. Repeat the layers one more time. Add the last one-third of the mushrooms and pour the sake over all. Cover with aluminum foil and bake for 35 minutes.

Mix the remaining 1 cup of breadcrumbs and the remaining one-third of the butter together and spread evenly on top. Bake, uncovered, for 10 minutes more.

Mu Shu Wood Ear Burritos (and Green Onion Sauce Brush)

"Buddha jumped over the fence" is how I describe a lighthearted transgression or moment of weakness like going off a diet. That was me during my ten years as a vegetarian, but I did my best to convert traditional meaty dishes to meatless. Mu shu wraps went veggie and I never looked back!

In a small bowl, soak the dried wood ear mushrooms in hot water until soft, about 15 minutes). Drain the water, then slice the rehydrated mushrooms into thin strips.

Pour 1 teaspoon of oil into a large skillet over medium heat and cook the eggs like an omelet. Transfer the omelet to a cutting board, cut into 2-inch strips, and set aside.

Turn the heat up to medium-high and pour in the remaining 1 teaspoon of oil. Stir-fry the garlic, ginger, green onions, salt, and white pepper for 15 seconds. Add the cabbage, celery, bamboo shoots, wood ear mushrooms, soy-ginger sauce, and sesame oil. Stir-fry 1 to 2 minutes, until the cabbage is slightly softened. Add the egg strips and toss about 1 minute or until heated through.

Warm up the tortilla wraps. This will take 30 seconds in the microwave or 1 minute in a steamer. Spread the hoisin sauce on one side of the tortillas, then fill each with ½ cup filling, top with crushed peanuts, and roll up to make the burritos.

For a fun serving idea, make a Green Onion Sauce Brush (page 81) for each guest and have everyone build their own burritos using the brush to spread the hoisin sauce.

Serves 4 to 6

1 ounce dried wood ear mushrooms

2 teaspoons vegetable oil, divided

2 large eggs, beaten

2 garlic cloves, smashed and minced

2 tablespoons grated ginger

2 green onions, julienned into 2-inch pieces

¼ teaspoon salt

¼ teaspoon white pepper

2 cups shredded napa cabbage

½ cup julienned celery

½ cup thin strips bamboo shoots

3 tablespoons Homemade Soy-Ginger Sauce (page 164)

1 teaspoon sesame oil

6 large spinach tortilla wraps or wraps of choice

¼ cup hoisin sauce

2 tablespoons crushed roasted peanuts or cashews

continued

Green Onion Sauce Brush

I encountered these cute and creative green onion sauce brushes at a fancy banquet dinner of Peking duck back in 1990. Each guest had their own "sauce brush," made from a green onion, to spread sauce on the roast duck (or mu shu) pancakes. If made with a large leek, they make great barbecue sauce brushes! Years later, in Taipei, my mom and I crashed an end-of-year employee appreciation banquet, known as *wei-ya* ("last tooth"), a soiree of round banquet tables sponsored by companies to thank employees for a year's worth of hard work and dedication. We saw these brushes being used to sauce up the celebratory dish that is associated with this occasion: pork belly bao buns, which inspired my Joy Luck BBQ Pulled Pork Bao Buns (page 132).

Makes 1 brush

1 whole stalk green onion
(or leek for a big brush)
Ice water

On a cutting board, cut off the hairy root end of the green onion. (Rinsed clean, these ends can be saved and used in a soup broth.)

On the white part closest to the end, use the tip of a sharp knife to make multiple lengthwise cuts, about 1 inch long, to resemble a brush. Trim off the stalk to the desired length (and use as a brush tie or add to a soup broth). I like to leave 2 to 6 inches of stalk to hold the brush.

To hold the brush together, tie a strand of excess stalk (or a colored ribbon, twist tie, or rubber band) around the uncut section just above the brush. Store in a bowl of ice water. The brush ends will curl up.

> *Note: Recycled food cans make good picnic table holders for these brushes. Wrap the cans in foil or recycled holiday or party paper to make them festive.*

Li'l Plates, Appetizers & Snacks

Most of the dishes in this section are associated with memories of outdoor excursions, like camping and kayaking at Lake Lanier, tubing on the Chattahoochee, or waterskiing on Lake Allatoona, where my dad could pull me with his bass boat as I was so petite. These days I throw a container of Harissa-Spiced Edamame Pods (page 96) into the cooler when we go on outings. The pods are biodegradable, so they don't create garbage. Jade Green Crunchy Okra (page 98), and Cracker-Crumb Chicken Nuggets with Hawaiian Mango Sauce (page 97) are also great take-along finger foods.

Whether we were headed for the cobblestones and beaches of Savannah or going to visit cousins in Cochran, the iconic peaches-and-peanuts stands along Georgia's highways provided as much fun as the destination. In sharing a boiled peanuts recipe, where my dad overlays his favorite Southern food with spices from his childhood, such as star anise and cinnamon (a stealthy flavor booster in Indian curries and Vietnamese pho), I hope to add a new dimension to the way Georgia peanuts bring joy to American palates. For our family, My Dad's Chinese-y Surprise Dirt Beans (page 85) conjures memories on both sides of the Asian-American aisle—fun road trips for us "native-born rascals," and for my parents, recollections of a "native" land that had long since begun to feel more foreign as their accents faded and they began to take on Southern drawls.

Seedy Pigs in a Blanket with Wasabi Mustard (page 89) are perfect for tucking into backpacks on day-long urban bicycling scavenger hunts, where participants like me get to know Atlanta's compelling history by riding through city neighborhoods, including Kirkwood, where my parents lived when they first moved to Atlanta. It was there, in a one-room apartment over a garage, that they, as proud but penniless new parents, repurposed a dresser drawer as a baby crib and snapped a black-and-white photograph to send to eagerly awaiting grandparents, some 8,000 miles away.

Before becoming a successful entrepreneur and real estate investor, my dad was a nuclear rocket scientist and inventor of the original helium pycnometer, a breakthrough instrument for analyzing industrial air pollution. Evenings would find him working overtime at the research lab at Georgia Tech, formulating heat transfer solutions for NASA. On summer date nights, he and my mom would fork out two dollars for dinner at the Varsity, hence the sentimental genesis of my Sweet Georgia Brown Fried Onion Rings (page 93). Then they would walk onto the freeway overpass, where she would point to a car driving by beneath them, and he would identify the make and model—free entertainment for her, bragging rights for him. Whether it was "nuclear rocket engine design" or optimizing moisture, texture, and taste for braised chicken wings, both were his pursuits of passion, precision, and perfection. His nuanced synthesis of zesty flavors would become the catalyst for my Flying Chicken Roasted BBQ Wingettes (page 94). Mouth-watering results and nothing short of rocket science.

A weekend bike ride in Atlanta's historic Kirkwood neighborhood, 1964. My dad with my oldest sister. (That's Dad's beloved VW Beetle.)

My Dad's Chinese-y Surprise Dirt Beans

My mom coined the name "Chinese-y Surprise Dirt Beans" ("dirt beans" is a direct translation of the colloquial Mandarin word for peanuts, or ground nuts). She loves boiled peanuts and Dad loved making them for her. I love them best hot or warm straight out of the slow cooker, cracking and slurping simultaneously to keep the hot brine from dripping down my wrists. Inevitably, my childhood overalls and shirts sported stains from boiled peanut brine. Luckily, I didn't get punished . . . because Mom's clothes were stained from eating hot boiled peanuts, too! Boiled peanuts are a traditional snack in China as well as in Georgia. Ever the chemist that he was, Dad loved trying out new twists to his peanuts recipe. Each new batch had a surprise ingredient, and guessing it right had my mama grinnin' like a possum. This recipe is my favorite flavor rendition—with an infusion of cinnamon and muscovado sugar—a match made in heaven, as he always said he and my mom were.

Serves 4 (or serves 1 if Mom gets a hold of 'em)

1 pound unshelled raw peanuts

¼ cup naturally brewed soy sauce

4 tablespoons muscovado sugar or 4 tablespoons dark brown sugar

1 tablespoon salt (optional)

2 cinnamon sticks or 1 teaspoon ground cinnamon

1 teaspoon minced shallot or 1 garlic clove, peeled and smashed

2 or 3 pods of star anise pods

In a large pot or bowl of water, soak the peanuts for 15 minutes to remove dirt. Rinse until the water runs clear and drain well. Dispose of any grit that has settled to the bottom of the pot.

If you would like to help the peanuts absorb more flavor in a shorter amount of cooking time, gently crack the tip of each peanut.

In a slow cooker, combine the peanuts, soy sauce, sugar, salt (if using), cinnamon sticks, shallot, and star anise pods. Add enough water to cover the peanuts. Put a heatproof plate on top to keep them from floating up during cooking. Cover and cook on high for about 6 hours, or to the desired tenderness. (We prefer the peanuts al dente rather than super soft. They're easier to remove from the shell that way, too.)

continued

Let the cooked peanuts cool in the pot with the seasoned liquid. Remove the peanuts from the pot with a slotted spoon. Crack open the shell and gently squeeze the peanuts out. Eat directly from the shell while slurping the liquid. Keep a hanky or towel handy and roll up your sleeves in case of dripping. (Discard the shells in the garden or a compost pile. Crushed peanut shells make a great mulch.) Cover any leftover peanuts with some of the seasoned liquid and store in the refrigerator. Consume within a week or freeze up to a month.

Note: To cook on the stovetop, mix all the ingredients in a large pot and pour in enough water to cover the peanuts. Bring to a boil, then reduce the heat to low and simmer for about 3 hours. Stir every half hour to allow the flavors to penetrate evenly. Add $1/2$ cup more water if needed to prevent drying out.

To cook in a pressure cooker, combine all the ingredients in the pot and add enough water to cover. Cook on high for 1 hour. Allow the pressure to release naturally and let the cooked peanuts rest for about 30 minutes in the seasoned liquid.

Black-Eyed Pea Hummus

The first time I ate hummus, in the college dining hall, I knew it would become a favorite—it's an easy, protein-rich staple to make as an appetizer or a light, nutritious meal with freshly cut vegetables for scooping.

Black-eyed peas are known as a Southern staple, but they originated in prehistoric China and proliferated in Southeast Asia (and are related to the mung bean). Enslaved West Africans brought it to the West Indies, as they did many of the Southern favorites we know now.

This is a great dip for parties, served with pita wedges or sliced veggies.

Serves 8 to 10 as an appetizer

2 garlic cloves, peeled
½ cup lemon juice
⅓ cup tahini
1 teaspoon ground cumin
½ teaspoon salt
½ teaspoon paprika
2 (16-ounce) cans black-eyed peas, drained
12 pita breads, quartered, for serving

In a food processor, blend the garlic until finely minced. Add the lemon juice, tahini, cumin, salt, paprika, and black-eyed peas and blend until smooth, scraping down the sides of the bowl as needed.

Serve chilled or at room temperature, with pita wedges.

Seedy Pigs in a Blanket with Wasabi Mustard

Mom was not into bread or sandwiches, but she loved hot dogs and sausages. After gobbling a dozen "pigs in a blanket" at a childhood sleepover, I decided to make them myself. This recipe was the closest thing we got to eating meat and bread together. It was also one of the few times we used our oven. The roasted sesame seeds add flavor to the rolls, and I still treat myself with these after workouts.

Serves 8

1 (12-ounce) package Pine Street Market Maple Bacon Breakfast Links or 10 to 12 petite smoked links of your favorite brand of sausage

1 (8-ounce) can crescent rolls (keep the dough refrigerated until ready to use)

1 tablespoon butter, melted

3 tablespoons toasted sesame seeds, for sprinkling

Wasabi mustard, for dipping

1 cup sweet mini gherkins (optional)

Preheat the oven to 375°F.

Cut each petite sausage link in half crosswise. On a lightly floured surface, separate the dough into 8 triangles along the perforation lines. Slice each triangle lengthwise in thirds, forming 3 narrow triangles.

Place a sausage piece on the short edge of a dough triangle. Roll up to the opposite point. On an ungreased baking sheet, arrange each rolled-up piece point-side down, a couple inches separating each piece. Brush each roll with melted butter and add a sprinkle of roasted sesame seeds.

Bake for 12 to 14 minutes, until golden brown. Remove from the oven, let rest for 5 minutes, and then gently remove the little pigs with a spatula. Serve warm with a side of wasabi mustard and sweet mini gherkins (if using).

Wasabi Deviled Eggs

When I was growing up, we had a lot of visitors come to our house—everyone from extended family to neighborhood kids—and we often had deviled eggs at these gatherings. They are a real Southern treat, not usually found on Asian menus, and my family took a liking to them right away.

Wasabi provides a touch of peppery pungency that adds balance to the mayonnaise in these deviled eggs. True wasabi isn't commonly eaten in the United States—here, wasabi is a horseradish. The milder Japanese root version is grated and eaten fresh.

Serves 12

6 large eggs
4 tablespoons mayonnaise
½ teaspoon Dijon mustard
½ teaspoon wasabi powder or
   1 teaspoon wasabi paste
1 teaspoon apple cider vinegar
Salt
Freshly ground black pepper
Smoked paprika, for garnish

Bring a pot of water to a boil. Turn the heat off and gently put the eggs in the water using a soup ladle. Turn the heat back on to high and cook the eggs for 12 to 14 minutes.

To make peeling the eggs easier, fill a medium bowl halfway with ice and water. After the eggs are done, transfer them to the ice water bath. Let the eggs cool completely, then peel and slice them in half lengthwise. Remove the yolks carefully with a spoon and put them in a medium bowl. Place the egg white halves on a plate.

To the bowl of egg yolks, add the mayonnaise, mustard, wasabi, vinegar, and salt and pepper to taste. With a fork, mash together the yolks and seasonings and mix until you get a smooth paste.

Add a small spoonful of the egg yolk mixture back into each egg white half. Garnish with a sprinkle of paprika. (I like Kentucky's Bourbon Barrel Foods Bourbon Smoked Paprika.)

Note: For an easy, homemade filling dispenser, scoop all of the egg yolk mixture into a quart-size plastic storage bag or a sandwich bag. Gently press and gather the mixture toward one corner of the bag. Snip off the tip of the plastic bag. Squeeze the yolk mixture into the egg white halves. Enlarge the hole if needed.

Home Alone
Garlicky Cilantro Yuca

I was introduced to yuca, also known as cassava, at a Peruvian restaurant where I was celebrating my graduation from Harvard. I fell in love with it. The presentation looked like boiled potatoes, so I found fresh yuca at the international market and went about making a homemade version without any recipe. I underestimated the pot size and water, but didn't think much of it since the yuca was soft and a little bitter. Undeterred, I just added more butter and garlic. Just in case, I looked up "yuca" and, to my horror, read that one variety was "deadly poisonous" and a small amount would kill a cow! I imagined the next day's headline: "Harvard Graduate Dies from Eating a Vegetable Enjoyed by Millions Around the World." Luckily, it all turned out okay!

This version is garlicky, so I don't recommend it for date nights—unless you want to share it! If you're up for extra potency, try it mojo style and don't cook the fresh garlic-onion mixture.

In a large pot filled halfway with water, add the frozen yuca and bring to a boil. Cook the yuca about 30 minutes, or until tender and a chopstick pokes all the way through. Drain. Let the yuca cool slightly, then cut roughly into 1-inch chunks. Put in a large bowl and set aside.

In a large pan over medium heat, combine the oil, garlic, ginger, red onion, and bell pepper. Sauté for 1 to 2 minutes, until the onion is softened and fragrant. Be careful not to burn the garlic. Stir in the salt, white pepper, and cumin, then pour the mixture over the yuca. Add the cilantro, lime juice, and orange juice and toss gently to coat and combine evenly. Adjust seasonings to taste and add the red chiles for a spicy kick, if desired.

Serves 4

1 (16-ounce) bag frozen yuca
¼ cup olive oil
4 garlic cloves, minced
1 teaspoon grated ginger
½ cup finely chopped red onion
¼ cup diced red bell pepper
½ to 1 teaspoon salt
¼ teaspoon white pepper
¼ teaspoon ground cumin
½ cup chopped cilantro
2 to 3 tablespoons lime juice (about 1 lime)
3 tablespoons orange juice
1 tablespoon chopped red chiles (optional)

Sweet Georgia Brown Fried Onion Rings

This is a tribute to the Varsity flagship restaurant in Atlanta, which has been in operation since 1928. The beloved local establishment is famous for its chili dogs and onion rings. My dad recalls eating there as a young Georgia Tech graduate student when a dollar would buy lunch.

If it's April through September, it's sweet onion bloomin' season in Vidalia, Georgia. Milder and sweeter than regular yellow or white onions, the one-and-only Vidalia sweet onions are perfect for snacking and for this recipe.

Peel and slice the onions ½ to 1 inch thick and separate the rings.

In a large bowl, whisk together the buttermilk and yogurt. Add the onion rings and coat them in the yogurt mixture. Cover and refrigerate for at least 1 hour.

In a 3-quart Dutch oven or heavy pot, pour peanut oil to a depth of 3 inches. Heat the oil to 365°F according to a food thermometer or test if the oil is ready by dipping a wooden chopstick in the oil and looking for oil bubbles around the tip.

In a wide mixing bowl or salad serving bowl, combine the flour, cornstarch, seasoning, and pepper in a wide mixing bowl. Using a fork, dredge the onion rings in the flour mixture until they are well coated. Add 1 ring at a time to the hot oil. Avoid overcrowding the rings. Fry in small batches for 2 minutes, or until the rings are golden brown.

Transfer the cooked rings to a wire cooling rack or a paper towel–lined plate. Mix a dollop of ketchup into the peach dressing and serve with and a dash of hot sauce (if using).

Serves 4

2 large Vidalia onions or other sweet onions
1 cup buttermilk
1 cup plain Greek yogurt
1 to 2 quarts peanut oil, for frying
2 cups all-purpose flour
1 tablespoon cornstarch
1 teaspoon Old Bay Seasoning
½ teaspoon white pepper
Ketchup, for serving
Homemade Sweet Chili Peach Dressing (page 161), for serving
Gochujang sauce, for serving (optional)

Flying Chicken Roasted BBQ Wingettes

Honey-braised chicken wings were always on my dad's menu at his chain of successful restaurants. Over thirty years, he ran ten restaurants around metro Atlanta. He was diligent about the quality of all the menu basics, including shrimp fried rice, barbecue wings, and handmade egg rolls with sweet iced tea. Our family always liked the parts of the chicken that had more bone—the wings or flats rather than the meaty drumette. In other parts of the world, I discovered later, the wings are considered a prime part, and thus a more expensive part of the chicken. In a funny play on words, the Mandarin translation for *airplane* sounds just like "flying chicken," so at some point, this became our nickname for the dish!

Shichimi togarashi is a Japanese seasoning blend with sesame seeds, orange zest, and ginger. It's optional for this recipe, but it will impart a toasty umami finish with a spicy zing.

Preheat the oven to 400°F. Using a pastry brush or a small piece of paper towel, lightly grease a baking sheet with vegetable oil.

In a ziplock bag or a large bowl with a lid, combine the flour, potato starch (if using), garlic powder, white pepper, and salt. Depending on the size of the wings, more than one bag may be needed. Add the chicken to the bag and shake briskly to evenly coat the wingettes. Refrigerate the bag of wings while you prepare the sauce.

In a small pan over low heat, melt the butter and coconut oil. Mix in the chili peach dressing, the teriyaki sauce, and the shichimi togarashi (if using). Transfer the sauce to a heatproof bowl. Using tongs, thoroughly coat each *wingette* in the sauce and lay out on the prepared baking sheet.

Bake for about 40 minutes, or until the chicken is crispy brown on the outside and reaches an internal temperature of 165°F. Halfway through the cooking time, flip each wing over to ensure even baking.

Makes 18 to 20 wings

½ teaspoon vegetable oil

⅓ cup all-purpose flour

2 tablespoons grainy sweet potato starch (optional)

½ teaspoon garlic powder

¼ teaspoon white pepper

½ teaspoon salt

2 pounds uncooked chicken wingettes or flats

3 tablespoons unsalted butter

1 tablespoon coconut oil

¼ cup Homemade Sweet Chili Peach Dressing (page 161)

¼ cup Homemade Teriyaki Sauce (page 165)

Shichimi togarashi (optional)

Harissa-Spiced Edamame Pods

Harissa is a North African and Moroccan blend of spices—paprika, caraway seeds, garlic, cumin, cayenne, and mild chiles—that works so well with edamame. These seasoned pods are a pop of spice in your mouth and make a great healthy snack.

When my mom was growing up in Taiwan, steamed edamame pods were often enjoyed at home, and sold as a popular movie snack in theaters. Mom said she devoured her favorite Jane Austen novels with a bowl full of edamame at her side.

Serves 4

1 (1-pound) bag frozen
    edamame pods
2 teaspoons salt
1 ½ teaspoons harissa powder
½ teaspoon dried oregano
½ teaspoon roasted sesame oil

In a medium or large pot, bring a pot of water to a boil. Put the edamame pods in all at once. The pods should be completely submerged. Boil until tender, 5 to 6 minutes. Drain in a colander.

In a small bowl, mix together the salt, harissa powder, and oregano. Sprinkle the seasoning mixture over the hot edamame pods and drizzle with the sesame oil. Toss well and serve warm.

Cracker-Crumb Chicken Nuggets with Hawaiian Mango Sauce

This recipe is a faster, lighter version of chicken nuggets, without a messy batter or marinating time. You can use plain, whole wheat, or seed crackers. Together with the cheese and herbs, you get added flavor and a light crunch without excess salt. I love it paired with the homemade Hawaiian Mango Sauce (page 161).

Serves 2 to 3 as an appetizer

Vegetable oil, for greasing
1 cup finely crushed
    cracker crumbs
⅛ teaspoon dried thyme
1 cup Parmesan cheese
2 boneless, skinless
    chicken breasts, cut
    into bite-size pieces
½ cup butter, melted
Hawaiian Mango Sauce
    (page 161), for serving

Preheat the oven to 400°F. Lightly grease a baking sheet with vegetable oil.

In medium bowl, mix the cracker crumbs with the thyme and Parmesan cheese. Dip the chicken pieces in the butter, then in the crumb mixture. Arrange on the prepared baking sheet. Bake until golden brown, about 30 minutes, flipping the nuggets halfway through the baking time. Serve with the mango sauce for dipping.

Note: To make in an air fryer, preheat the fryer on 400°F for 3 minutes. After dipping the chicken pieces in the crumbs, spray them with a little vegetable oil and put them in the preheated air fryer. Cook the nuggets 4 to 5 minutes, or until light brown on one side. Turn the chicken pieces over and cook for another 4 to 5 minutes or until light brown. If needed, cook 1 to 2 minutes longer, until the chicken reaches the desired level of crispiness.

Jade Green Crunchy Okra

Inspired by the adage that less is better, sometimes you need to meet an okra on its own terms. You don't slice, dice, fry, or season this (other than salt). It is a crunchy, not slimy, way to enjoy a healthy alternative to fried okra. I remember a neighbor calling okra "ladies fingers," and I later found out that's what they call it in other parts of the world, especially in the Philippines and India.

In a 3-quart saucepan half-filled with water, add the salt and sesame oil and bring to a boil. Add the okra and blanch until the okra turns bright green, about 2 minutes. Test 1 piece for desired crunchiness. For softer okra, continue boiling for 1 more minute.

Remove the okra and rinse under cold water. Arrange on a serving plate and serve with your choice of dipping sauce.

Serves 4

1 teaspoon salt
$\frac{1}{2}$ teaspoon roasted sesame oil
24 fresh whole okra pods
Daikon Radish Dipping
    Sauce (page 152) or Thai
    Memories Macadamia
    Nut Dressing & Toss Sauce
    (page 154), for serving

Noodles, Salads & Slaw

Going to Vassar College in New York exposed me to new holidays and traditions, beyond Easter and Christmas. I met classmates who were kosher, vegan, lacto-ovo, pescatarian, and "granola heads." Every mealtime became a fascinating microcosm of world cuisines, with socio-political discourse transpiring over blintzes, tabbouleh, and ugali. Cream cheese and jelly on matzo bread became a favorite snack. In exchange, I enlightened them on the difference between Cream-of-Wheat and grits and what "devil" meant in the South when talking about eggs, crab, and chocolate cake (or Sunday sermons). These myriad eat-this-try-that experiences engendered many of the concepts that culminated in my own creations, such as Japchae-Inspired Glass Noodles with Swiss Chard (page 107) and Dinosaur Kale & Asian Pear Salad (page 108).

In the early sixties, confronted with segregated lavatories, my dad had to ask which bathroom to use. Unfortunately, a generation later, racial tension reared its ugly head again, when my sister showed me a flyer that was left on her car windshield after shopping at the mall with her "white" boyfriend: MIXED COUPLES GO TO HELL. Fast-forward to the present: The need to disguise myself in American flag t-shirts and sunglasses in public, to avoid anti-Asian harassment and anti-immigrant sentiment, is yet again a sobering reminder that, unlike a moonshine hangover, pervasive prejudice won't disappear on its own, without courage, intentionality, and action.

To get away from ethnic labeling, I saw moving to New England as a way to "escape" from the South and a chance to fit in with the "liberal Yankees." But things didn't turn out as I expected. Being elected vice president of the Asian Students Union was very disorienting—was I now being validated and empowered for the identity that I had tried so hard to leave behind? Organizing the first all-campus, multicultural Race Dialogues led to my selection to Who's Who Among Asian Americans and my appointment to the Governor's Task Force Against Hate Crimes. For the first time, I could be Asian and Southern and fit in—and make a difference.

Years later, I would again share my stir-fry tips, but this time as a featured presenter at the Cook's Warehouse in Atlanta. They enjoyed my demos and liked me, but they loved my mom, an adorable glamour queen with a master's degree in English literature, brandishing a cleaver, turbo-chopping vegetables, and captivating audiences with her philosophical East-West humor. Though often pegged as a "tiger mom" because she looked the part, people quickly realized she was a perpetually cheerful and fun-loving Tigger-mom. At the Cloister exclusive hotel at Sea Island Resort, we headlined a five-star weekend of sea-to-table events, which inspired the seafood filling for my Kawaii Calamari Twice-Fried Gyoza Fritters (page 27).

There was no looking back. Instead of running away, I leaned in, drawing strength and support from my Asian American brothers and sisters while reaching out across the table to bridge divides. Embracing my newfound hybrid identity, I found my own voice at the junction of my Asian heritage and my American vision, and it prepared me for the next step in my journey—taking on leadership roles in public service.

Mom and I created the first-ever series of cross-cultural workshops and hands-on Asian cooking classes. "What kind of musicians do dumplings love?" "Wrappers." Mom's jokes kept them laughing. And the food kept them craving more.

Sweet Chili Peach Napa Slaw

This recipe is dairy-free because I was allergic to milk when I was little. The sauce is inspired by a natural duck sauce that my family made at home. I like using napa cabbage instead of regular cabbage because it's lighter, better absorbs the sauce, and is easy to slice into thin strips. This slaw is nutritious and affordable, and I like to make it as a side dish for picnics and a topping for sliders.

In a large bowl, whisk together the chili peach dressing, vinegar, sesame oil, soy sauce, and white pepper.

Add the cabbage, red and orange bell peppers, snow peas, and green onions to the sauce and combine. Add salt to taste.

Garnish with Mandarin orange segments, toasted cashews, peanuts, or a sprinkle of roasted sesame seeds.

Serves 4 to 6

¼ cup Homemade Sweet Chili Peach Dressing (page 161)

3 tablespoons rice vinegar

2 tablespoons roasted sesame oil

1 tablespoon naturally brewed soy sauce

1 teaspoon white pepper

3 cups finely shredded napa cabbage

1 red bell pepper, thinly sliced

1 orange or yellow bell pepper, thinly sliced

½ cup thinly sliced snow peas

3 green onions, thinly sliced

Salt

Mandarin orange segments, toasted cashews, peanuts, or sesame seeds, for garnish

Sour Green Mango & Peach Salad

My mom had wild mango trees in Taiwan and loved them, though the fruit was small, fuzzy, and a little sour. She would climb up on the roof with her brother to pick them! I love Georgia peaches, so I came up with this salad to please both of us. Peaches are native to China, where they are a delicacy—especially white peaches—and revered in paintings and artwork.

I love cilantro so much that I eat cilantro as a vegetable and frequently add it to salads. If you don't like cilantro, you can substitute chives.

To prepare the mangoes, slice off the flesh in 1 large piece on each side of the large pit, perpendicular to the pit. Holding 1 mango half in hand, carefully score the mango through the flesh—but not through the skin—with a sharp knife in a crosshatch pattern. Using a large spoon, scoop the mango chunks out from the peel. Repeat with the other half. Cut off the peel around the pit and slice off the extra flesh for the salad. If using a green mango, peel it with a peeler and cut into thin matchsticks or shred with the big hole side of a grater.

In a large bowl, thoroughly combine the mangoes, peach, green onion, bell pepper, sugar, Tajín, lime juice, peanuts, cilantro, mint, salt to taste, and chile (if you want a spicy kick). Adjust the salt and seasonings to taste depending on how sweet or tart the fruit is.

Serves 4

1 ripe mango
1 green mango, or
    another ripe mango
1 fresh, firm peach,
    peeled and sliced
1 green onion, finely chopped
⅓ cup thinly sliced red
    bell pepper
1 teaspoon sugar
1 teaspoon Tajín Clásico
    Chile Lime Seasoning
1 teaspoon lime juice
1 cup roasted peanuts
⅓ cup chopped cilantro
1 teaspoon minced mint
Salt
1 red chile, minced (optional)

Korean-Style Garden Potato Salad

When I visited Korea, I enjoyed sandwiches using potato salad as a sandwich filling. It's a side dish (or *banchan*, in Korean) for Southerners, but I like it as a meal, too.

I like less gooey potato salad with more crunch, so the celery gives it a nice fresh garden taste. Eat in season using the Georgia-grown Honeycrisp apples, or substitute Fuji apples if you don't have the Honeycrisp variety. For a low-fat version, use Greek yogurt instead of mayonnaise.

Serves 3 to 4

1 pound red potatoes, skin on, halved
2 ¼ teaspoons salt, divided
1 cup water
½ cup peeled and diced carrots
½ English cucumber (about a 5-inch-long segment)
1 Honeycrisp apple
¼ cup chopped celery
½ cup mayonnaise
1 tablespoon sugar
1 teaspoon white pepper
2 hard-boiled eggs, diced

Fill a large pot halfway with water and bring to a boil over high heat. Add 1 teaspoon of salt and add the potatoes. Boil for 15 to 20 minutes, until the potatoes are soft enough to mash. Test a piece at 15 minutes. Drain the liquid and mash the potatoes.

Bring a small pot of water to a boil over high heat. Add the diced carrots and boil until tender (but not mushy), about 5 minutes. (Alternatively, steam in a microwave-safe bowl on high for 2 minutes.) Drain.

Slice the cucumber into very thin semicircles. Put the sliced cucumbers in a medium bowl and toss well with ¼ teaspoon of the salt. Set aside for 10 minutes to release the excess water. Wash off the salt in cold water, gently hand-squeeze the excess water out of the cucumbers, and set aside. Reserve the salt brine in a small bowl for the apples to prevent browning (or store in the refrigerator as a starter for pickling recipes).

Peel and cut the apple into ½-inch cubes. Place the apple cubes in the reserved salt brine from the cucumbers. Set aside. When ready to mix into the salad, strain the apples and discard the brine.

In a medium salad bowl, mix together the mashed potatoes, carrots, apples, celery, and cucumber slices. Add the mayonnaise, remaining 1 teaspoon of salt, sugar, and white pepper. Mix well until combined. Add the diced eggs and mix gently, until all the ingredients are combined. Adjust the seasonings as needed.

Shape and serve with an ice cream scooper as a side dish or on top of a salad. Enjoy immediately or chilled.

Japchae-Inspired Glass Noodles with Swiss Chard

I was an early fan of Korean japchae, then had the chance to travel to Seoul and became an even bigger fan. Traditionally, sweet potato noodles are used in japchae. They are slightly thicker and chewier than bean thread noodles. I use mung bean thread noodles, also called cellophane or glass noodles, in my version because they were easier to find in small-town international grocery outposts when I grew up. Mung bean noodles are a refreshing, less filling, and gluten-free alternative to traditional flour noodles.

Prepare the bean thread noodles by pouring the water over the noodles in a large bowl. Let stand 15 to 20 minutes or until al dente.

While waiting for the noodles to soften, make a sauce by mixing together the soy sauce, brown sugar, honey, vinegar, and sesame oil in a small bowl.

Drain and rinse the noodles under cold water for 1 minute to cool them off and prevent them from sticking.

Heat the vegetable oil in a large skillet or wok over medium heat. Add the green onions, garlic, and ginger and stir-fry for 30 seconds to season the oil. The ingredients should sizzle and be fragrant but not brown. Add the yellow onion, carrot, bell pepper, mushrooms, and chard and stir-fry 1 to 2 minutes, until the vegetables are al dente and the greens are slightly wilted. Add the noodles and sauce. Mix everything together and toss for another minute in the hot pan so that the noodles are evenly coated with the sauce. Garnish with the seeds, cilantro, and chili paste (if using). Serve hot or cold—it's delicious both ways.

Serves 2

- 3 small bundles (4 ounces each) bean thread or glass noodles
- 4 tablespoons naturally brewed soy sauce
- 1 tablespoon brown sugar
- 1 tablespoon honey
- 1 teaspoon black vinegar or balsamic vinegar
- 2 tablespoons roasted sesame oil
- 2 tablespoons vegetable oil
- ¼ cup sliced green onions
- 2 garlic cloves, minced
- 1 tablespoon grated fresh ginger
- ½ cup thinly sliced yellow onion
- 1 cup julienned carrot
- ½ cup thinly sliced red bell pepper
- 4 shiitake mushrooms, stems removed and thinly sliced
- 2 cups chard or spinach leaves, sliced
- 1 tablespoon roasted sesame seeds, for garnishing
- ¼ cup chopped cilantro, for garnishing
- 1 teaspoon hot chili paste or hot sesame oil, for garnishing (optional)

Dinosaur Kale & Asian Pear Salad

I never met a kale (or for that matter, a *Brassica* family member) that I didn't like. Kale is easy to grow and grab from a home garden and readily available at farmers' markets. Hardy enough to withstand chilly weather, and versatile enough for hot or cold dishes, any variety of kale is my lazy-cook, grab-a-green, fall and winter superfood staple. Dinosaur kale is a little softer and sweeter than the curly kale variety, so it's perfect for salads. Asian pears are sweet, crisp, and juicy. They may be a little harder to find, but it's worth the effort.

In a large bowl, whisk together the lemon juice, dressing, oil, and salt. Add the kale and toss well. (If you used hardier curly kale, let it marinate for 10 minutes.) Add the dates, pear, almonds, feta, and pecorino and toss well. Season with salt and pepper to taste.

> *Note: To make this salad a meal, top with grilled seafood, cooked slices of marinated beef, sautéed chicken strips, or pan-seared tofu.*

Serves 6

2 tablespoons fresh lemon juice

2 tablespoons Homemade Sweet Chili Peach Dressing (page 161)

2 tablespoons extra virgin olive oil

¼ teaspoon sea salt

1 bunch dinosaur (lacinato) kale, ribs removed and chopped (about 2 cups)

¼ cup chopped dates, raisins, or dried cranberries

1 Asian pear, sliced

¼ cup sliced roasted almonds

¼ cup crumbled feta cheese

¼ cup finely grated pecorino cheese

Salt

Freshly ground black pepper

Savory Miso-Butter Garlic Noodles

I love miso—I enjoy it in soup, like a rub, or as a savory seasoning for everything from turkey to broccolini. I love how these noodles are flavorful and stand on their own, yet are versatile enough to complement almost any type of vegetable or protein. Miso adds a light umami touch without being overpowering, plus it has healthy probiotics. Play around with different noodles. Treat yourself or impress friends with an easy, elegant dinner by topping the noodles with Seven-Spice Lemon Garlic Georgia Shrimp (page 139).

Cook the pasta according to the package instructions.

When the pasta is done, reserve 2 tablespoons of hot pasta water before draining. To avoid sticking, rinse and toss the pasta in a colander under cold water for 30 seconds. Return to the pot or a bowl, toss with 2 tablespoons of olive oil, and set aside.

In a medium bowl, dissolve the miso paste completely in the hot pasta water. Add the soy-ginger sauce, mirin, sesame oil, and sriracha and mix well. Set aside.

In a large wok or pan, melt the butter, then add the remaining 2 tablespoons of olive oil, the garlic, and the shallots. Sauté over the lowest heat for 5 to 8 minutes, until the garlic is fragrant and soft. (The garlic should stay light-colored; fresh garlic burns easily, so remove the pan from the heat immediately if the garlic starts to brown on the edges.)

Add the cooked pasta, chives, cilantro, and the miso sauce to the wok. Toss everything together. Keep tossing and turn the heat up to medium for 1 minute to heat everything through.

Garnish with sesame oil and chili flakes (if using). Serve warm.

Serves 4

1 pound spinach linguine

4 tablespoons olive oil, divided

1 teaspoon miso paste (light or dark)

¼ cup Homemade Soy-Ginger Sauce (page 164) or soy paste

2 tablespoons mirin

1 tablespoon roasted sesame oil, plus more for garnish

1 teaspoon sriracha

3 tablespoons butter

5 garlic cloves, minced

¼ cup finely chopped shallots

½ cup chopped fresh chives

½ cup chopped fresh cilantro

Chili flakes, for garnish (optional)

Mom's Chinese Spaghetti

Say "spaghetti" and kids' eyes light up. Even kids who speak non-English languages to their grandparents. So for my birthday party one year, my mom made spaghetti—well, her version of it. "Mine's better. It has my 3 Gs. Your friends will love it." I grappled with the thought of my middle-school classmates "loving" spaghetti that, one, wasn't orange, and two, contained three "eew" aromatics: green onion (eew), ginger (double-eew), and garlic (triple-eew). But my mother was right. They loved it. Their parents loved it. Our neighbors loved it. Friends and family loved it. It's a standout go-to for birthdays when the candle-blower is sixty or older, because long (uncut) noodles auspiciously signify long life.

In a 12-inch skillet over medium heat, heat 1 tablespoon of canola oil. Add the garlic, ginger, and chopped green onions and sauté for 1 minute. Increase the heat to medium-high and add the ground meat. Using the back of a spoon or a flexible silicone spatula, stir while breaking up the clumps and sautéing the meat until it is no longer pink.

Add the ground bean sauce, hoisin, black pepper, and ¼ cup of water and stir to combine into a saucy meat mixture. Add the vegetables to the mixture and simmer, uncovered, for 25 minutes over medium-low heat. If desired, add another ¼ cup of water and stir occasionally until the vegetables are softened and have absorbed the meat sauce mixture in color and flavor.

Meanwhile, cook the noodles according to the package instructions and drain. Serve the hot meat sauce over the noodles and drizzle with the sesame oil. Garnish with sliced green onions (if using).

Serves 4

2 tablespoons canola oil, divided

4 garlic cloves, minced

2 to 3 tablespoons finely chopped ginger

½ cup finely chopped green onions

1 pound ground beef, pork, or a mix

⅓ cup Asian-style ground bean sauce

¼ cup hoisin sauce

1 teaspoon freshly ground black pepper

¼ to ½ cup water, as needed

1½ cups finely chopped or shredded mixed vegetables (shredded cabbage, chopped celery, chopped unpeeled zucchini)

1 (16-ounce) box whole wheat thin spaghetti or Cantonese-style egg noodles

1 to 2 tablespoons roasted sesame oil, for drizzling

Sliced green onions, for garnishing (optional)

Moon over Wasabi: 1-Minute Avocado Scoop & Dip

This dish salutes multicultural Miami as a melting pot of palates. The gargantuan Florida avocado is mildly flavored, versatile, and more filling than the more popular, petite Haas avocado. I leave it au natural, perfectly paired with the star in this simple dish: real wasabi—Wasabi Japonica, if you can find it. Genuine wasabi is notoriously difficult to cultivate and is a rare culinary delicacy, even in restaurants in Japan. Wasabi Americana does not contain true wasabi root. Enjoy this fresh, nutritious, good-fats snack without washing dishes, precision, or pretension. Most of all, kudos to the humble horseradish for most outstanding performance by a spicy root-vegetable understudy.

Serves 1 to 2

1- to 1 ½-pound Florida avocado or 2 to 3 Haas avocados
1 tablespoon tamari
¼ teaspoon wasabi paste, Americana or Japonica
1 teaspoon local Sourwood honey or honey of choice
Meyer lemon wedge, for squeezing (optional)

Cut the avocado in half and carefully remove the pit. In a small bowl, mix the tamari, wasabi, and honey until well combined and smooth. Add a squeeze of Meyer lemon (if using) for a tangy, ponzu-like flavor.

Pick your favorite eating spoon (not for measuring!). Scoop up a spoonful of avocado and dip the very tip of the spoon and avocado into the sauce mixture. Savor the flavor as the avocado melts in your mouth . . . and your worries away. Sometimes, I just stand at the counter, spoon in hand, ready to scoop and eat. Have a quasi-wasabi blast for a day.

Spicy Pig Ear Salad

There's a little barbecue joint on Memorial Drive in Atlanta where we always have to stop for my mother's favorite melt-in-your-mouth pig ear plate with a side of collards and the best spiced sweet potatoes. If you snooze, you lose—they often sell out.

By popular demand, my Asian food tours and cooking classes now cover sticky rice balls, as well as congee, thousand-year-old egg, stinky tofu, and pig's feet. I hear there's a Disgusting Food Museum in Sweden. As I chew on my pig's knuckle, I'm also chewing on why 65 percent of the foods on the infamous list are from Asia and none are from North America. Now, that's food for thought (and the best pig's feet in town).

Put the pig ears in a large pot and pour in just enough water to submerge them. Add the ginger, green onion, chiles, and 1 teaspoon of salt and boil over high heat for about 20 minutes. Remove the pig ears and set them on a cutting board to cool. Cut into small strips along the gristle line and transfer to a serving plate.

In a small bowl, whisk together the chili oil, sesame oil, stock, remaining 1 teaspoon of salt, vinegar, sugar, soy sauce, and sesame seeds until the sugar dissolves. Pour the sauce over the pig ear strips on the serving plate. Garnish with chopped green onions and cilantro.

Serves 2 to 3

3 pig ears, prewashed or washed according to the package instructions

3 (⅛ inch thick and 2 inches in diameter) slices ginger

1 green onion, cut into 4 or 5 pieces

3 whole dried red chiles

2 teaspoons salt, divided

1 tablespoon hot chili oil

1 tablespoon roasted sesame oil

3 tablespoons chicken stock or water

1 teaspoon balsamic vinegar

1 teaspoon sugar

1 tablespoon naturally brewed soy sauce

1 teaspoon roasted sesame seeds

Chopped green onions, for garnishing

Fresh cilantro, for garnishing

Buddha Bubba, Meat & Bones

Raising us kids in the South in the region known as the "Bible Belt" could be challenging, and my parents did their best to strike a balance and highlight the best of East-West traditions. As an adult, I jokingly started referring to my stories and essays about growing up as an Asian American in the Deep South as "Buddha-Bubba" stories and lessons. At home, remember your heritage. At the restaurant, don't argue with customers when they call fortune cookies a Chinese food. At school, raise your hand and ask questions (a no-no in strict Chinese classrooms). At summer camp, make new friends—and learn the lyrics to "Found a Peanut" so you can sing along on the bus. They also placed importance on being mindful of social mores that were endemic to the South. Not saying *ma'am* or *sir* when responding yes or no to an adult was a capital offense, and my mother always kept her toenails painted (and she still does—to understand the significance of this, ask a born-and-bred Southern woman).

As an adult Georgian, I notice food and cultural intersections everywhere. Many ethnic groups prefer dark meat, which results in chicken thighs being more expensive than chicken breasts at international grocery stores. We have a running family joke about chicken thighs. Every Thursday, there's a drive-through special on a bucket of chicken thighs at my dad's favorite fried chicken outlet. One time, my oldest sister and I went to get some for him. While waiting, we chitchatted with the drive-though lady. She bragged about how good their fried chicken thighs were. We agreed and told her we were going to surprise my dad. "My dad loves your thighs," I said. Though technically true, that remark came out embarrassingly wrong. We apologized and got out of Dodge as fast as we could, hugging our bucket of thighs and wiping tears of laughter from our eyes (Fried Chicken Spring Rolls with Honey on page 20 commemorates that incident).

The saying "nothing is new under the sun" seems to apply to some food habits. What seems like the hot new food trend in the United States might be recognized as hundred- or even thousand-year-old traditions in another culture. Such is the case with bao buns, which are juxtaposed with a Southern favorite, pulled pork, in Joy Luck BBQ Pulled Pork Bao Buns (page 132). Pork is naturally flavorful, versatile, and easy to prepare, with plenty of natural moisture and fat, making it more forgiving on cooking time. The bao bun sandwiches combine the savory, smoky flavors of slow-cooked pork with tangy crunchy slaw, and I love that the pineapple and Hong Biou Michiu quality-controlled Taiwan rice wine in I-Lava-You Island Chunky BBQ Sauce with Pineapple & Coconut Sugar (page 160) will double as natural meat tenderizers.

In Whole Silkie Black Chicken Soup (page 121), the chicken takes center stage, but here, it's the supporting actors who steal the show. Even the ensemble—in aggregate—play a critical role. In the first stage of cooking, the large-cut vegetables, durable herbs, and strong aromatics create a conducive environment for extracting the essence of this black-boned, black-skinned bantam. In the second phase, the ensemble—hominy, garlic chives, and mushrooms—step up for the grand finale, enveloping classic American vegetables in perfect harmony. Don't be embarrassed if the chicken feet, neck, or head turn you off. My mom doesn't like them either, and even I still sometimes get squeamish.

We were campground gourmets, because we brought mom's 3Gs (garlic, ginger, green onion) and sauces in our cooler—and extra long bamboo chopsticks.

Sweet & Sour Stir-Fried Meatballs

Most people make meatballs in a slow cooker, but this recipe uses a wok and a skillet. You can cook the meatballs in the skillet while you're stir-frying the vegetables in the wok, then add them to the wok at the end. It cuts the cooking time immensely.

In a large bowl, mix together the ground meat, wine, 1 tablespoon of cornstarch, the flour, the egg, and the green onions. Stir until well blended and sticky. Form the meat mixture into 1-inch meatballs.

In a large skillet over medium-high heat, heat 1 tablespoon of vegetable oil. Brown the meatballs in 1 layer (or in batches, if needed) on at least 2 sides, cooking about 2 minutes per side. Remove the meatballs from the heat and set aside.

In a small saucepan, whisk together the soy sauce, sugar, vinegar, A.1., water, and remaining 1 tablespoon of cornstarch until smooth. Bring the mixture to a boil. Pour the remaining 1 tablespoon of vegetable oil into a large wok and heat over medium-high heat. Add the mixed vegetables and stir-fry until al dente, about 2 minutes. Add the meatballs and the sauce to the vegetables. Toss for 1 minute until coated evenly. Serve hot.

Serves 4

1 pound ground pork or beef

2 tablespoons red wine

2 tablespoons cornstarch, divided

1 tablespoon flour

1 large egg

¼ cup finely chopped green onions

2 tablespoons vegetable oil, divided

⅓ cup naturally brewed soy sauce

⅓ cup sugar

¼ cup balsamic vinegar

2 tablespoons A.1. Sauce

½ cup water

2 cups sliced mixed vegetables (such as carrots, mushrooms, broccoli florets, etc.)

Whole Silkie Black Chicken Soup

A nourishing Asian Silkie, slow-simmered with all-American vegetables, perfectly complements cilantro, an ancient herb that, for thousands of years, has connected civilizations as a popular cooking and medicinal herb. To avoid too much of a meaty overtone, I rely on the old-timey kitchen hack of using a chopstick to keep the pot's lid slightly propped open (keep adding water so the chicken stays submerged). It's a bit more work, but the two-stage process of cooking the broth, then "rebooting" the soup from scratch, really makes a huge difference. There are a lot of steps, but they're all easy. For someone worthy of some TLC, making them some homemade soup says "I care." The priceless ingredient that can't be substituted is time. Silkie chickens are sold frozen online and in international supermarkets.

For the first stage, prepare the ingredients to make the broth base. Drain the hominy and rinse well. You can blanch the hominy for 1 minute in a small pot of boiling water to slightly soften it. Drain and refrigerate.

If the cilantro still has roots attached, remove and discard them. Gripping several stalks tightly with both hands, twist to separate the stems from the leaves. Remove any defective leaves and thoroughly wash the stems and leaves, removing all traces of dirt and sand. Dry in a salad spinner or pat between kitchen towels. Refrigerate in a storage container lined with a folded paper towel. Cut the garlic chives into ½-inch segments, making about ¼ cup. Set aside or refrigerate (to preserve flavor).

Rehydrate the dried shiitake mushrooms by soaking them for at least 10 minutes and up to 40 minutes, stems facing down, in the hot water. While the shiitakes rehydrate, strip the sprigs of thyme, separating the stems from the leaves (about 1 tablespoon).

Put the thyme stems, 4 ginger slices, and the onion quarters in a 5-quart soup pot or Dutch oven. The pot must be large enough for

Serves 4

1 (15-ounce) can hominy

1 bunch cilantro

2 stalks garlic chives

2 dried shiitake mushrooms

1 cup hot water

2 sprigs fresh thyme, stems and leaves divided

1 large unpeeled knob (3 to 4 ounces) ginger, cut into 6 slices, divided

1 onion, quartered

3 whole carrots, greens top and knob ends removed, divided

3 celery stalks, leaves removed, divided

1 large shallot

1 (2-pound) Silkie chicken

1 teaspoon sea salt

¼ teaspoon freshly ground black pepper

½ teaspoon naturally brewed soy sauce

2 fresh shiitake mushrooms

1 cup finely diced red pearl onions

1 tablespoon extra virgin olive oil

¼ teaspoon white pepper

continued

the chicken and all the vegetables to fit inside without touching the lid when covered.

Peel 1 carrot and cut into 3 segments. Cut 1 celery stalk into 3 segments as well. Add the carrot and celery segments to the pot, shifting them to the sides and leaving room in the middle for the whole chicken.

Remove the softened shiitakes from their soak, reserving the water. Using kitchen shears, remove (and keep) the stems, snip each mushroom into quarters, and add to the pot. Rinse off the cilantro stems one more time and add them, uncut, to the pot. Do not add any of the leaves yet. Peel and halve the shallot and set aside.

Rinse the chicken, inside and out. Remove the head, neck, and feet using kitchen shears and/or a cleaver. Place the head, neck, and feet inside the cavity for extra flavor when cooking, or discard. Stuff the shallot into the cavity, then put the chicken in the pot. Pour in enough water to completely submerge the chicken, with about ½ inch of water at the top. Add the sea salt, black pepper, and soy sauce.

Over medium-low heat, simmer the chicken broth for 20 minutes. During those 20 minutes, clarify the broth by using a small fine-mesh strainer (or a ladle) to skim off any froth that rises to the surface. (Frothing or foaming is a natural occurrence when making bone stock. Although the froth is referred to as *scum*, it is merely coagulated proteins and, contrary to popular belief, doesn't contain any harmful impurities.)

After clarifying the broth, slowly pour the shiitake mushroom water into the pot, discarding the last ounce or so to avoid pouring in any sandy residue at the bottom. Cover the pot, wedging a wooden chopstick between the pot and the lid to keep the lid propped open slightly. Continue to simmer the stock for another 2 hours.

While the broth simmers, prepare the soup vegetables needed for the second stage of cooking. Slice the fresh shiitakes to about ¼ inch thick. Peel and finely dice the remaining 2 whole carrots, and finely dice the remaining 2 celery stalks.

After 2 hours of simmering time, use a fork to see if the meat comes off the bone. If so, turn off the heat and continue with the next steps. If not, simmer for an additional 30 minutes before turning off the heat.

Using tongs, remove the larger vegetable segments. Then, using a spider strainer or slotted ladle in one hand and an inverted wooden spoon in the other, lift the chicken with the strainer and insert the spoon's handle into the chicken cavity. Carefully lift the chicken out of the pot and transfer it to a large mixing bowl. Allow the chicken to cool for 10 minutes. Meanwhile, strain the soup with a fine-mesh strainer and return the clear broth to the pot. Discard the strained solid content, or better yet, add it to the garden compost. Add the remaining 2 ginger slices to the broth.

For the second stage of the soup, turn the heat to medium-low and begin reheating the strained broth. Like before, cover the pot and use a chopstick to keep the lid slightly propped open. Adding one ingredient at a time, gently stir in the hominy, garlic chives, diced carrot, diced celery, fresh shiitakes, and pearl onions.

From the mixing bowl, remove the 2 drumstick bones and put them back into the soup pot, as they will continue to impart flavor. Debone the rest of the chicken by pulling the meat off with your hands or a fork, keeping all or just some of the skin (if desired). Shred or cut the chicken meat into bite-size pieces and set aside. Discard the remaining bones and unwanted skin.

Finely mince the thyme leaves and add them to the shredded chicken with the olive oil and white pepper. Mix to combine. Spoon the chicken back into the soup and continue simmering over medium-low for 40 to 50 minutes, without letting the soup come to a full boil. Once the vegetables are tender, serve in bowls and garnish with the cilantro leaves.

Turkey Burger Sliders on Grilled Rice Buns

Spice up your next barbecue or party with this creative, Japanese-inspired gluten-free "bun" as an alternative to traditional wheat buns. The oats help tenderize the burger meat. You can substitute breadcrumbs for the oats, or add one egg.

Though often discarded or considered optional, I view burger toppings and sauces as essential show-stoppers. Tomatillos are one of my favorites—if you pick them, know that they are sweetest when they have fallen to the ground. Topped with a fresh slice of garden tomato, tomatillo, and drizzled with Homemade Sweet Chili Peach Dressing (page 161), Homemade Soy-Ginger Sauce (page 164), or Homemade Teriyaki Sauce (page 165), this turkey goes uptown from plain to gourmet!

To make the rice buns: Pour the cooked rice out on a baking sheet to cool for about 20 minutes. With a wet spatula or hands lightly coated with vegetable or sesame oil, press and form the cooked rice into an even solid 1-inch-thick layer. Cut out 16 slider-size (3-inch) circles with the top of a clean, empty jar, soup can, or dough cutter.

In a small bowl, combine the cornstarch, garlic powder, and salt, then pour onto a plate. Pat each side of the rice patties in the dry mix.

In a frying pan over medium-high heat, heat the oil. Fry the rice patties until golden brown on both sides. Garnish with roasted sesame seeds (if using).

To make the burgers: In a blender or food processor, grind the oats into a powder.

In a medium bowl, mix the turkey, ground oats, onion, red pepper, soy sauce, ginger, garlic powder, onion powder, and black pepper together until well combined. Form into 8 equal-size patties. Grill or panfry the burgers over medium-high heat until brown on both sides and cooked through (to an internal temperature of 165°F). Remove the burgers from the heat immediately to avoid drying out the meat.

Serve the turkey rounds in between the rice buns with a slice of fresh tomato, tomatillo, and a drizzle of your sauce of choice.

Makes 8 sliders

FOR THE RICE BUNS
3 cups cooked sushi rice (medium-grain Japanese rice)
½ cup cornstarch
½ teaspoon garlic powder
½ teaspoon salt
Vegetable oil, for frying
1 tablespoon roasted sesame seeds (optional)

FOR THE BURGERS
⅓ cup instant oats
1 pound ground turkey
½ cup finely chopped yellow onion
½ cup finely chopped red bell pepper
2 tablespoons naturally brewed soy sauce
1 tablespoon grated fresh ginger
1 teaspoon garlic powder
1 teaspoon onion powder
1 teaspoon freshly ground black pepper
Sliced tomatoes and tomatillos, for serving
Homemade Sweet Chili Peach Dressing (page 161), Homemade Soy-Ginger Sauce (page 164), or Homemade Teriyaki Sauce (page 165), for serving

Papaya-Pineapple Baked Chicken

Papaya and pineapple are superfoods and natural meat tenderizers; their fruit enzymes break down the collagen in meat. I created this recipe for the White Oak Pastures farm. Over the years, I featured their chicken in our cooking classes and shared the story of their farm and humane treatment of their flavorful, pasture-fed chickens. Thighs and drumsticks don't need tenderizing. If you substitute chicken breasts, marinating the chicken in yogurt for 30 minutes will help tenderize the meat.

Preheat the oven to 350°F.

On a plate or in a shallow bowl, combine the flour and seasoned salt. Dredge the chicken pieces in the mixture to coat and place on a plate or small tray. Cover with plastic wrap and put the coated chicken in the refrigerator to marinate for 30 minutes.

Pour the melted butter into a baking pan. Arrange the chicken, skin-side down, in the pan. Top with pineapple rings, reserving the juices, and bake for 40 minutes.

While the chicken is baking, in a small saucepan over medium heat, mix together ½ cup of reserved the pineapple juice, brown sugar, oyster sauce, salt, and cornstarch. Cook until thickened. Gently stir in the papaya.

When the chicken is done baking, pour the sauce over the chicken, return the pan to the hot oven, and bake for another 10 minutes. Serve hot with rice or mashed potatoes.

Serves 3 to 4

1 cup flour

1 teaspoon seasoned salt

2 pounds skin-on chicken pieces, boneless thighs or drumsticks

½ cup butter, melted

1 (15-ounce) can pineapple rings

¼ cup brown sugar

2 tablespoons vegetarian oyster sauce or Homemade Soy-Ginger Sauce (page 164)

½ teaspoon salt

1 teaspoon cornstarch

1 cup bite-size pieces papaya or mango

Prepared rice or mashed potatoes, for serving

Rum Pao Chicken with Zucchini

Few dishes are famous enough to have their own bio. Kung pao chicken is one of them. Legend has it that, as a child, a *kung pao* ("protector of the prince") named Ding fell into the river and was rescued by a farmer. When Ding later visited the farmer's family to express his appreciation for saving his life, they served him a spicy diced chicken dish chock-full of peanuts, and kung pao ji ding was born. The homophonic play on his name, which, together with the word *ji*, for chicken, sounds like diced chicken, minted the legend and the man to this popular dish.

The one downside to this dish, for me, is the lack of vegetables, so I was delighted to discover that a somewhat limp zucchini in my fridge and a cup of peanuts, plus a splash of this and that, elevated a couple of chicken thighs to hey-I'm-onto-something level. The addition of Richland Rum (the only single-estate, single-source rum distillery in the country) just makes it all the better, but be ready to scarf down two bowlfuls of rice with this dark and savory chicken! For faster cooking preparation, dice the chicken the day before and marinate overnight. For freezer meal prep, you can freeze the marinated chicken for a week or for up to one month by tucking the ziplock bag into a recycled foil (chips) bag.

In a quart-size ziplock bag (or recycled bread bag), seal the chicken pieces, 1 tablespoon of rum, 1 tablespoon of soy sauce, the salt, a good grind of black pepper, and 4 teaspoons of cornstarch. Massage to coat thoroughly, and set in the refrigerator to marinate for 20 minutes.

Prepare the cooking sauce by whisking together the remaining 1 tablespoon of rum, the remaining 3 tablespoons of soy sauce,

Serves 4

1 pound boneless, skinless chicken breast, diced into ½-inch pieces

2 tablespoons Richland rum or rum of choice, divided

4 tablespoons naturally brewed soy sauce, divided

½ teaspoon salt

Freshly ground black pepper

6 teaspoons cornstarch, divided

3 tablespoons water

½ cup Coca-Cola

1 tablespoon mirin or sugar

2 teaspoons balsamic vinegar

6 tablespoons peanut or vegetable oil, divided

2 dried red chiles, seeds removed, cut into ½-inch pieces

2 teaspoons minced garlic

1 tablespoon roasted sesame oil

2 cups diced zucchini

1 cup extra-large premium Virginia peanuts or peanuts of choice

Steamed white or brown rice, for serving

the remaining 2 teaspoons of cornstarch, water, cola, mirin, and balsamic vinegar. Set aside.

Add 3 tablespoons of the peanut oil to the marinated-chicken bag and massage in before frying—this will help the pieces separate more easily during cooking.

In a wok or heavy skillet, heat the remaining 3 tablespoons of peanut oil over medium-high heat. Sauté the chicken until the surface of the meat is cooked and no longer pink (medium well). Use a spatula to move the pieces to the sides of the wok, creating a hole in the middle.

Put the red chiles, garlic, and sesame oil in the center of the wok and stir to combine. Add the zucchini and peanuts and stir-fry the chicken with the vegetables for about 1 minute. Pour in the sauce mixture. Cover and cook for 30 more seconds until steam escapes from the edge of the wok.

Uncover and gently stir one more time to mix everything evenly.

Serve over steamed white or brown rice.

Georgia Bourbon & Coca-Cola Meatloaf

This recipe calls for half pork and half beef, which adds a combined richer flavor and more tenderness than using ground beef alone. Dad's meatloaf recipe had a secret ingredient: old-fashioned Coca-Cola (which contained real sugar, not high-fructose corn syrup, also referred to as "Mexican Coke"). Back then, without social media or the internet, I'm not sure where he got the idea, but he was always experimenting with mystery or secret ingredients. Of course, Atlanta was the birthplace of Coca-Cola. The origins of ketchup ("ket-chap" or "ke-tsiap" in the Hokkien dialect), similar to Worcestershire sauce, can be traced back to 300 BC China and south Asia and began as a fermented fish sauce, sometimes with added flavors of cinnamon, clove, and tamarind. No wonder I like it so much! I like to use farm-raised meat from Riverview Farms and Brasstown Beef in Georgia, and Georgia Bourbon Whiskey from Moonrise Distillery, but you can substitute your favorite brands.

Preheat the oven to 350°F. In a small bowl, soak the crackers in the milk for 5 to 10 minutes.

In a large bowl, combine the beef, pork, onion, carrot, garlic, egg, 2 tablespoons of ketchup, cola, bourbon, Worcestershire sauce, pepper, garlic powder, and the cracker mixture. Using your hands or a serving fork, combine well.

Spread the meat mixture in an even layer in a loaf pan.

In a small bowl, mix together the teriyaki sauce, remaining ¼ cup of ketchup, brown sugar, and dry mustard. Spread the sauce evenly to coat the top of the meatloaf.

Bake, uncovered, for 50 to 60 minutes. Remove from the oven and let the meatloaf rest for at least 10 minutes before slicing. Spoon extra teriyaki sauce on top before serving, if desired.

Serves 2 to 4

1 cup crushed saltine crackers

½ cup milk

½ pound ground beef

½ pound ground pork

½ cup finely chopped sweet onion such as Vidalia

⅓ cup grated carrot

1 garlic clove, minced

1 large egg, beaten

¼ cup plus 2 tablespoons ketchup, divided

2 tablespoons Mexican Coca-Cola or regular Coca-Cola

2 tablespoons Georgia bourbon whiskey

1 teaspoon Worcestershire sauce

½ teaspoon freshly ground black pepper

½ teaspoon garlic powder

¼ cup Homemade Teriyaki Sauce (page 165), plus more for serving (optional)

1 tablespoon brown sugar

1 teaspoon dry mustard

Game-Day Five-Spice Sausage Meatballs with Teriyaki Glaze

Football rivalries in the South are intense. Game-day food will delight fans, but do they calm competitive impulses? Probably not. I use Homemade Teriyaki Sauce (page 165) and a locally made sausage in this recipe along with rice instead of breadcrumbs to help tenderize the meatballs. Just a touch of five-spice powder complements the meat—it's very potent, so just a smidgen is perfect.

In a large bowl, mix together the sausage, green onions, cilantro, ginger, garlic, honey, sesame oil, rice, soy sauce, cooking wine, pepper, and five-spice powder. Shape into about 25 (1-inch) meatballs and place on plates or a baking sheet.

In a medium bowl, whisk the cornstarch and 2 tablespoons of the teriyaki sauce until smooth. Add the rest of the sauce to the cornstarch mixture and whisk until smooth; set aside.

In a large skillet over medium-high heat, heat the vegetable oil. Brown the meatballs in a single layer (or in batches) on at least 2 sides, cooking about 2 minutes per side. Pour in the sauce mixture and gently coat the meatballs in the sauce. Bring to a boil for about 1 minute. Toss again, then turn the heat down to medium-low, cover, and cook for another 10 minutes. Remove the lid and let it simmer, uncovered, for 5 minutes. Toss again with the thickened sauce. Arrange the meatballs on a serving dish with toothpicks, sprinkle with toasted sesame seeds, and serve hot.

Serves 4

1 pound ground mild breakfast sausage
¼ cup finely chopped green onions
¼ cup finely chopped fresh cilantro
1 tablespoon minced fresh ginger
1 tablespoon minced garlic
1 teaspoon honey
1½ teaspoons toasted sesame oil
½ cup cooked rice, white or brown
½ tablespoon naturally brewed soy sauce
1 tablespoon Shiaoxing wine or cooking sherry
1 teaspoon freshly ground black pepper
⅛ teaspoon five-spice powder
1 teaspoon cornstarch
1 cup Homemade Teriyaki Sauce (page 165)
2 teaspoons vegetable oil
Toasted sesame seeds, for garnish

Note: If using a slow cooker or multi-cooker, brown the meatballs in a pan first or with the multi-pot's sauté function. Pour the sauce mixture over the meatballs in the cooking pot, cover, and set to low or the slow cook function. Cook for 2 hours, stirring every 30 minutes. Add a little water if needed (in case of game overtime!) or add extra sauce, if desired.

Grandma's Teriyaki Pork Chops

My paternal grandmother, or nai-nai, was from the countryside in Shanxi province and grew up very poor. She told us stories about enduring wartime rationing, how frugality became a way of life, and how she learned to make tasty meals with only scant ingredients.

We had an after-school routine when I was young. She would often make me these teriyaki pork chops and serve them with celery sticks and ketchup—regardless of where they are from, I think all children like ketchup! Together we would watch two television shows: *Let's Make a Deal* (no English understanding required) and *The Flintstones* (no common sense required). Every day as I ate, she would point out, "You are a lucky girl, Natalie, to have good food." I heartily agree.

In a small bowl, combine the soy sauce, garlic powder, honey, and ketchup to make a marinade. Place the pork chops in a dish, pour the marinade over the top, cover the dish with plastic wrap, and marinate for at least 20 minutes at room temperature, or refrigerate if you choose to marinate longer.

When you are ready to cook the chops, set a large skillet over medium heat and pour in the oil. Arrange the chops in the pan so they do not touch, cover, and cook for 6 to 8 minutes, then turn and continue to cook, covered, another 6 to 8 minutes, until both sides are browned.

Serve with celery sticks and ketchup or teriyaki sauce on the side, for dipping.

Serves 2 to 4

⅓ cup naturally brewed soy sauce

1 teaspoon garlic powder

2 tablespoons honey

2 tablespoons ketchup

4 small bone-in pork chops

2 tablespoons vegetable oil

Celery sticks, for serving

Ketchup, for serving (optional)

Homemade Teriyaki Sauce (page 165), for serving (optional)

Joy Luck BBQ Pulled Pork Bao Buns

We always had company over. The gatherings were year-round, from the Fourth of July and Thanksgiving (open door policy) to NCAA March Madness and the Tour de France. They were never potlucks because Mom insisted on making everything homemade, from a five-course meal or a table full of tapas to her creative eco-friendly decorations (that's a used lightbulb?). Bao buns are usually sold frozen. Just steam according to the package instructions. This recipe can be easily scaled up for a group dinner or tailgating. Go Braves!

Prepare the pork by trimming off excess fat and taking out the bone. In a 6-quart slow cooker, combine the pork and BBQ sauce, cover, and cook on low for 8 to 10 hours. Transfer the pork to a cutting board and shred with 2 forks. Return the pork to the cooker and mix well with the sauce; keep warm.

In a skillet on high heat, pan-grill the pineapple slices until slightly browned with marks, about 2 minutes per side. Set aside. (This step is optional but highly recommended.)

To serve, spoon pulled pork onto the bottom of each bun, top with slices of onion, slaw, and a slice of grilled pineapple, and sprinkle with chopped cilantro. Cover with the top bun and enjoy.

Serves 8

1 (4-pound) bone-in pork shoulder

4 cups I-Lava-You Island Chunky BBQ Sauce (page 160)

1 fresh pineapple, peeled and sliced into rings

8 bao buns or 16 slider-size buns (such as King's Hawaiian sweet rolls)

1 recipe prepared Sweet Chili Peach Napa Slaw (page 103)

½ Vidalia onion, julienned

4 ounces (2 bunches) fresh cilantro, chopped

Vidalia Onion Burgers

Burgers and steaks were my family's favorite thing. It was a special treat to go out, and as the baby of three daughters and the one who suffered severe food allergies as a toddler, I usually got to pick where we would eat. My favorite place was the Ponderosa Steakhouse, and I always ate my burgers there with A.1. Sauce. I love the versatility of this recipe, incorporating Vidalia onions and my Homemade Teriyaki Sauce (page 165). The sweet Vidalia onion is grown only in Vidalia, Georgia. A milder, sweeter cousin of yellow or white onions, it's perfect for eating raw or chopped up in a burger. Enjoy this Southern Asian twist on an American classic!

In a skillet over medium heat, heat the oil and brown the onion for 3 to 5 minutes, until translucent. Remove from the heat and let cool to room temperature.

In a large bowl, mix the cooked onion with the egg, soy sauce, ginger, garlic, cornstarch, and white pepper. Combine with the ground meat, using your hands to get a uniform mixture of the seasonings. Using ½ cup of meat, form 6 slider patties and grill or panfry for 5 to 7 minutes, until browned on both sides.

On a grill or in a skillet, toast the buns quickly. Serve the patties on the toasted buns with a squeeze of the teriyaki sauce. Add sliced tomatoes, cheese, onion, and lettuce to serve.

Serves 6

1 tablespoon vegetable oil
½ cup chopped Vidalia onion
1 large egg, beaten
¼ cup naturally brewed soy sauce
1 teaspoon minced ginger
1 teaspoon minced garlic
1 teaspoon cornstarch
1 teaspoon white pepper
1 ½ pounds ground beef, turkey, or a mix
⅓ cup Homemade Teriyaki Sauce (page 165)
6 mini slider buns
2 fresh tomatoes, sliced
Sliced cheese, for serving
Sliced onion, for serving
Lettuce, for serving

Drunken Ginger All-Purpose Asian-y Minced Pork Filling

This is an easily tweakable recipe that I have kept secret for many years. It wins accolades when enjoyed with my award-winning sauces at tastings. It wins hearts young and old when tucked into dumplings, potstickers, and wontons from any Asian cuisine, including Cantonese shumai, Japanese gyoza, and Korean mandu (and even ravioli!) at birthday parties and reunions. Tinged with a splash of Kentucky bourbon, the convergence of aromatics of white pepper, garlic chives, and ginger in this versatile filling parlays a light and delicate flavor. This recipe is enough for a half pack of standard store-bought wrappers or a batch of Preppy Pink & Green Handmade Dumpling Wrappers (page 31).

Refrigerate the finely chopped garlic chives while preparing the ground meat.

Using a fork, mix the water into the meat to keep it from over-binding. Slightly beat the egg white and mix it into the meat. Add the soy sauce, bourbon, ginger, sesame oil, salt, white pepper, and dashi powder (if using) and stir to mix thoroughly. Fold in the finely chopped chives.

Tuck the mixture into wrappers in 1- to 2-teaspoon portions. Wrap and cook one as a taste test, then adjust seasonings as needed.

Makes 20 to 25 dumplings

1 cup finely chopped garlic chives, gently packed

2 tablespoons water

1 ¼ pounds (25 to 30 percent fat) ground pork

1 egg white

2 tablespoons naturally brewed soy sauce

1 tablespoon Kentucky bourbon, or bourbon of choice

1 teaspoon finely minced ginger

½ teaspoon roasted sesame oil

½ teaspoon sea salt

¼ teaspoon white pepper

½ teaspoon dashi powder (optional but recommended)

20 to 25 dumpling wrappers

Gone Fishin'

My parents loved nighttime fishing with a lantern on the lake dock. We kids would play games and sleep in the back of our station wagon. Sometimes, other fishermen would give us their catch, complaining the specific variety was too bony and not good eating. We never turned down free fish—my scrounge- and-save parents saw it as free nutrition!

I have included a heritage whole-fish recipe and detailed every step in the hope that it will motivate some first tries. Although the instructions look dauntingly wordy, in practice, the wok-frying method that I use for Auspicious Fish: Banquet-Style Whole Pompano (page 142) isn't that hard once you get the knack of it and is suitable for various types of fish that can be cooked whole (generally), 1- to 1 ¼-pound whitefish—ocean or fresh, wild-caught or farmed, whichever is most sustainable and environmentally friendly.

On the other end of the spectrum is Late-Night Fish Sticks Congee (page 149), an ode to the headless, tailless, boneless form of fish that harkens back to public school lunches. A visit to Tainan, a southern coastal city in Taiwan where fish is so abundant it's even eaten for breakfast, led me to transpose frozen fish sticks into a congee (rice porridge) topping.

On our annual family vacation to Panama City, Florida, we had to get up really early for the 8- to 10-hour drive. Baggie-friendly handheld foods, like Pan-Grilled Rice Bun Sliders (which debuts here with a grown-up filling of Salmon & Creamy Chili Crisp Aioli [page 141] but used to be canned tuna for us kids) make great in-the-car breakfasts, for both kids on trips and commuters stuck

Top: Have overalls, will fish (and, will eat whole). I loved munching on the crisp-fried fins and tails. Never met a fish I didn't like.

Bottom: Mom made her own dough-ball fish bait. I once ate some, thinking it was fudge. When we went trout fishing in the South Island, New Zealand, the guide said these two beauties were only medium in size. We were thrilled nonetheless.

on GA-400. The road trip was part of the fun. I Spy and two renditions of "A Hundred Bottles of Beer on the Wall" usually got us about halfway to "Are we there yet?" Our station wagon would inevitably cruise back to Atlanta with a car full of tired, sunburned kids, wet beach towels, and our fishy, crabby, shrimpy cargo on ice.

Speaking of shrimp, Georgia has the best shrimp in the world, hands down, and I have a true fish tale to prove it. My dad once took some out-of-town visitors to go fishing and crabbing. On the way, he stopped at the bait shop to buy a bucket of live shrimp. After that trip, he returned home empty-handed. "We didn't catch any fish," he said, which was implausible, and he knew I needed a full explanation. "The guests ate all the bait!" No kidding—the shrimp were boiled and eaten plain, because they were "so sweet they didn't need any sauce."

Seven-Spice Lemon Garlic Georgia Shrimp

Don't be bamboozled by the simplicity of this savory shrimp recipe. As nutritious as they are delicious, Georgia shrimp are uniquely chubby, sweet, and juicy, and carry the shichimi togarashi's matrix of flavors to a level of eloquence that belies the effortlessness of this dish. So if the weekend is coming up and you're in need of a magical "cheat" for a date night, or your in-laws have a tendency to "drop by" without notice, grab a couple of pounds of peeled, deveined shrimp, some fresh snow peas (or sugar snap peas), and a pack of nice pasta noodles. I pair this dish with Savory Miso Butter Garlic Noodles (as shown) and some Sautéed Lemon Pepper Snow Peas (page 59). They're sure to be impressed, and only you will know it was as easy as falling off a log.

In a large skillet over medium heat, melt the butter and olive oil. Stir-fry the garlic for 30 seconds. Increase the heat to medium-high and add the shrimp. Stir-fry the shrimp until pink and heated through, about 3 minutes. Add the lemon zest, lemon juice, shichimi togarashi, and sea salt. Toss to coat the shrimp in the seasonings. Garnish with the cilantro and serve immediately.

Serves 3 to 4

2 tablespoons butter

2 tablespoons extra virgin olive oil

4 garlic cloves, minced

1 pound medium to large shrimp, peeled and deveined

Grated zest and juice of 1 lemon

½ teaspoon Japanese shichimi togarashi

1 teaspoon Beautiful Briny Sea's French Picnic Sea Salt, or sea salt of choice

¼ cup chopped cilantro, for garnishing

Hot Hunan Catfish Fillets

Catch-and-clean and catch-and-eat were family fishing tenets, and gobs of my mom's 3 Gs—ginger, garlic, and green onion—were ever-present items in our camp cooler. My mom never met a fish she couldn't cook. However, there is one fish dish that she never makes herself and never opts out of when it's on a restaurant menu: fried catfish. It's her all-time favorite, and she has eaten it in at least a dozen seafood shacks and shanties across the South. As in many Southern kitchens, there is always some Old Bay Seasoning in our pantry, so it's a familiar taste to match catfish. But, for a Japanese-inspired twist, I like to use shichimi togarashi, a widely available mixed chile seasoning that goes all the way back to the seventeenth century Japan and typically features seven ingredients: red chile pepper, sansho pepper, white or black sesame seeds, poppy seeds, ground ginger, orange or yuzu peel, and nori. For convenience, frozen catfish fillets work perfectly, and for a bit of reduction on fat and calories, I've switched from a FryDaddy to an air fryer for preparing this dish.

Serves 4

3 medium eggs
1 tablespoon full-fat Greek yogurt
½ teaspoon salt
½ teaspoon sesame oil
2 tablespoons shichimi togarashi
1 ½ cups flour
2 cups Japanese panko breadcrumbs
2 pounds catfish fillets
Vegetable oil, for coating
Hot Hot Hunan Fresh Chile Sambal (page 159), for serving

In a medium bowl, beat together the eggs, yogurt, salt, and sesame oil for at least 1 minute, or until well blended and frothy; set aside. In another medium bowl, mix the shichimi togarashi into the flour; set aside. Pour the breadcrumbs into a third bowl.

Cut the fillets into 2 x 3-inch pieces (about the size of a business card). Roll one fish fillet in the flour mixture to thoroughly coat both sides. Dip in the egg mixture, then coat with breadcrumbs. Repeat for the remaining fillets in the first batch, 4 pieces at a time. (This is how many fillets will fit in the air fryer at once.)

Preheat the air fryer at 360°F for 4 minutes. Lightly coat the fillets with oil using a brush or oil mister. Place the fillets in a single layer in the air fryer basket or tray and cook for 7 to 9 minutes at 400°F. Using tongs, gently turn the fillets over and brush or spray each piece lightly with more oil. Continue cooking for another 4 to 5 minutes or until golden and crisp. Repeat with the remaining batches. Drizzle with chile sambal to serve.

Note: If catfish is not available, wild-caught cod or halibut steaks are worthy pinch-hitters. Just be sure to thoroughly dry the fillets before cooking. Old Bay Seasoning is more salty but can be substituted for shichimi togarashi.

Pan-Grilled Rice Bun Sliders with Salmon & Creamy Chili Crisp Aioli

Spice up your next party with this creative, Japanese-inspired gluten-free alternative to burgers and bread buns. The rice buns are fried so they hold together better, but that won't be a problem for long; these small sliders are gone in three or four bites.

To make the rice buns, pour the cooked rice out on a baking sheet to cool for about 20 minutes. With a wet spatula or hands lightly coated with vegetable or sesame oil, press and form the cooked rice to an even solid 1-inch-thick layer. Cut out 12 slider-size (3-inch) circles with the top of a clean, empty jar, soup can, or dough cutter.

In a small bowl, combine the cornstarch, garlic powder, and salt, then pour onto a plate. Pat each side of the rice patties in the dry mix. In a frying pan over medium-high heat, heat the oil and fry the rice buns until golden brown on both sides.

To assemble the sliders, place a piece of smoked salmon on one bun and top with a cucumber slice and a smear of aioli. Pop another bun on top and garnish with roasted sesame seeds (if using).

Makes 6 sliders

3 cups cooked sushi rice (medium-grain Japanese rice)

½ cup cornstarch

½ teaspoon garlic powder

½ teaspoon salt

Vegetable oil, for frying

1 (3- to 4-ounce) package smoked salmon

½ English cucumber, peeled and sliced into thin rounds

¼ cup Creamy Chili Crisp Aioli (page 156)

1 tablespoon roasted sesame seeds (optional)

Auspicious Fish: Banquet-Style Whole Pompano

Believe it or not, I once caught a pompano and stirred up quite a ruckus, because it's usually a surf-fishing catch, and I was fishing off a pier. In Taiwan and many other Chinese-speaking countries, whole pompano is frequently the fish of choice for wedding banquets as well as Lunar New Year's Eve dinner. Wholeness auspiciously connotes completeness in marriage and having the whole family gathered together to celebrate the beginning of a whole new year. When cooking this dish, the key is to dry the fish thoroughly inside and out, to pat off all excess flour when dust-coating, and to keep the frying temperature right around 350° to 360°F to ensure thorough cooking. Tender and delicate in flavor yet firm enough to not fall apart while cooking, whole pompano, on a large platter lined with kale and adorned with cherry tomatoes, makes for a fancy presentation dish on special occasions, or, as we say in the South, when you're having company for supper.

To make the sauce, pour the olive oil into a small saucepan over medium-low heat. Add the grated ginger, garlic, the white parts of the green onions, and the chopped cilantro stems. Stir-fry for 2 minutes, until fragrant, then add the sesame oil, vinegar, mirin, cane sugar, honey, white pepper, ketchup, soy sauce, wine, and hot sauce. Cook and stir for another 2 to 3 minutes, until the mixture boils. Remove from the heat and transfer to a microwave-safe spouted bowl. Set aside.

Rinse off the fish. Using paper towels, thoroughly dry the fish, including around the head, gills, fins, and abdominal cavity (to do this, stuff paper towels inside, press gently, and then pull out the towels). Let the fish air-dry for about 10 minutes on a wire rack with a baking sheet underneath.

Preheat a wok over medium-high heat for 3 to 4 minutes. While the wok is heating up, firmly grasp the ginger knob and carefully rub the cut surface of the ginger all over the inside of the wok (wearing a glove-style oven mitt is recommended, as the wok is very hot).

Serves 4 as a banquet dish,
    2 as a dinner main dish

2 tablespoons olive oil

2 teaspoons grated ginger

3 tablespoons finely minced garlic

3 green onions, finely chopped,
    white and green parts separated

1 tablespoon finely chopped
    cilantro stems

1 teaspoon roasted sesame oil

2 tablespoons apple cider vinegar

2 tablespoons mirin

2 tablespoons cane sugar

1 teaspoon honey

¼ teaspoon white pepper

¼ cup ketchup

2 tablespoons naturally
    brewed light soy sauce

2 tablespoons local white,
    red, or rosé wine

1 teaspoon sriracha or
    gochujang sauce

1 (1-pound) whole pompano fish
    or whole whitefish of choice

1 (1- to 2-inch) knob
    unpeeled ginger

½ cup vegetable oil

½ cup all-purpose flour

4 to 5 whole kale leaves,
    for plating (optional)

3 tablespoons chopped cilantro
    leaves, for garnishing

6 to 8 cherry tomatoes,
    for garnishing

continued

This step is optional, but my po-po always said it helps keep the fish from sticking. Set the ginger knob aside for later use. Pour the vegetable oil into the heated wok.

While the oil is heating to full temperature, between 350°F and 365°F (this will take 5 to 7 minutes), prepare the fish. For the fancy version, trim the tail by cutting away a "V." I don't trim the dorsal or pectoral fins because it makes the connecting bones less visible, and pulling away the fin while eating is the easiest way to remove those little bones along the top. Making sure your hands are dry, dust and pat the fish with flour on both sides, including the head and the tail. Be generous with the flour, then firmly pat or shake off any excess so you have a thin layer.

Using a large knife, make several slits (about 1 ½ inches apart) along the body of the fish, cutting at an angle, until the knife hits the bone—don't cut through the bone. Leave about a 1-inch margin of uncut skin between the slits to the edge of the fish. Repeat the slits on the other side of the fish. Some home chefs will score the fish in a checkerboard pattern, but a pompano isn't very thick, so a few slits, even two, will do for cooking purposes, unless you have some reason to gussy it up (such as for social media or a special dinner guest).

Gently place the fish in the hot oil. Using a spatula to hold the fish in place, gently tip the wok so the oil coats the head and tail. For even cooking, repeat this step every few minutes. Do not attempt to move the fish. Fight the temptation and don't mess with it. After 1 minute, turn the heat down to medium and cover with a splatter screen. Fry the fish for 4 to 6 minutes. During this time, cut the ginger knob into slices, then cut the slices into little sticks and carefully drop them into the oil around the fish.

Shake the wok gently. If the fish moves or shifts around, it is ready to be turned. Using 2 spatulas (or a spatula and a pair of extra-long cooking chopsticks or a wooden spoon), carefully turn the fish over. The cooked side of the fish should be golden brown. If not, finish cooking the second side, then flip again. Fry for

continued

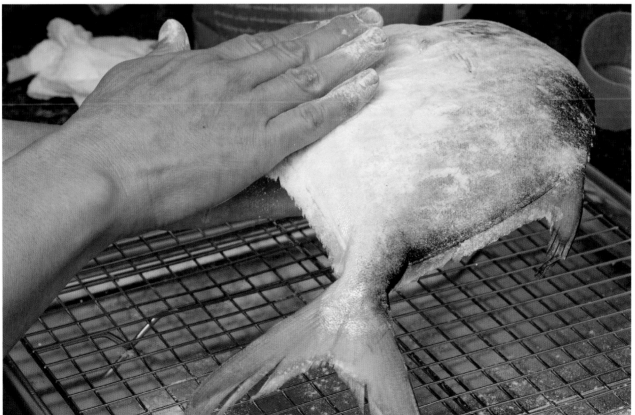

another 3 to 4 minutes, or until the whole fish is golden brown on both sides.

Prepare a large serving platter or plate. For a banquet-style presentation, line the platter with the kale leaves. To crisp the fish skin, turn the heat to high and let the fish fry for about 1 minute. The oil will begin to sizzle and might splatter a bit. Carefully remove the fish from the oil and place it on the serving platter.

Stir the green parts of the green onion into the sauce and reheat in the microwave in 10-second intervals, stirring after each interval, 30 to 40 seconds total. Carefully pour the sauce over the fish. Some folks (like me) like to smother the whole fish with sauce. Others prefer to pour a little over the middle section and leave the head and tail showing. Garnish with the cilantro and cherry tomatoes.

Late-Night Fish Sticks Congee

With Georgia being home to thirty lakes and four thousand miles of trout streams, there was always fish in our house. But no such thing as a fillet—no, when it came to fish, it was head-to-tail. Like riding a bike, I was trained early on how to eat whole fish without choking on the bones (chew carefully with very small swallows). Bone-free fish never made so much as a cameo appearance on our dinner table. Well, lucky for fourth-grade me, fish sticks were a public-school "delicacy" that appeared every now and then as the main course on our lunchroom menu—next to a blob of tangy tartar sauce or ketchup, in those sectioned trays. Yum.

Serves 1

½ cup bone broth of choice
½ cup vegetable broth
1 cup leftover Base Camp White Rice with Quinoa (page 41) or cooked white rice
2 to 3 frozen fish sticks
1 tablespoon chopped cilantro stems or green onions
Salt
White pepper
Ketchup or other sauce of choice, for dipping

To make the congee, in a small saucepan over high heat, bring the bone and vegetable broths to a boil. Turn off the heat and immediately add the rice. If the rice is chilled, add it before turning off the heat. Stir gently to combine. Cover and let sit for 1 to 2 minutes.

In the meantime, microwave the fish sticks for 30 seconds, then flip and heat in 20 second-increments until hot, or prepare according to the package directions.

Give the congee a brief stir, then ladle it into a bowl. Top with the fish sticks, garnish with the greens, add salt and white pepper to taste, and drizzle with ketchup or sauce of choice. Serve immediately. For a thicker consistency, let the congee rest for up to 20 minutes (the rice will puff), to achieve the desired consistency, then top with the fish sticks and serve. The longer the congee sits, the thicker it gets.

Note: Cilantro can be washed and chopped in advance, then frozen in recycled foil-lined tea-bag sleeves, single serving chip/snack bags, or small ziplock bags. Defrost before using or add to a hot pot of soup or congee.

Gettin' Saucy

Believe it or not, there was a time I didn't like to eat. Maybe I was still traumatized from severe food allergies as a baby (a diagnostic prick-test showed that I was allergic to more than fifty foods—thank my lucky stars I outgrew *that*). Year after year, I was the shortest kid in my grade, hence always front-and-center in class photos, since we were lined up by height. Apparently trying to make up for lost meals and make-believe dinner parties, instead of a Play-Doh maker, I asked Santa for a stove. Instead of a Barbie, I asked for a baby doll that ate food (or pretended to).

I am the founder and owner of a small business that makes nothing but sauces. Sauces make everything better, don't they? Even though upholding high standards of quality, like being all-natural, using fresh rather than powdered ingredients, and avoiding cheap fillers like high-fructose corn syrup, poses challenges from higher small-batch production costs to shelf-life concerns, I don't want to sell anything that I wouldn't give to Grandma or eat myself, especially since some of the recipes, including Homemade Soy-Ginger Sauce (page 164), were inspired by her cooking. All of the sauces must pass the Grandma test and, after taste testing in the local school district cafeterias, also be kid approved!

To my delight, my sauces have earned many enthusiastic fans, from ages one to one hundred and from many different backgrounds. And apparently, the fans are sometimes more innovative than I am when using my sauces. My dad concocted his Bloody Sweet Hottie Cocktail (page 194) by adding my Homemade Sweet Chili Peach Dressing (page 161) to a shot of vodka. My Indian neighbors drizzle my Homemade Teriyaki Sauce (page 165) onto their samosas and pakoras, and Hot Hot Hunan Fresh Chile Sambal (page 159) on hot dogs. I try to make sure each of my sauces is truly a premium, authentic recipe in and of itself—a natural blend of a dozen fresh ingredients and spices all in one bottle, so when you shake it up, you're cookin' up a storm. The one complaint I get is that using my sauces turns you into a lazy cook!

Daikon Radish Dipping Sauce

Most of us don't buy vegetables with a split in them, but in a radish, that's a good sign. It means it's juicy and tasty! When peeling a daikon radish, be sure to remove enough skin to reach the tender inside. To check, cut a section of the radish and examine the surface of the circular cross-section to make sure no white rim remains after peeling. Try this dipping sauce with Jade Green Crunchy Okra (page 98).

Serves 4

3 tablespoons local wildflower honey
½ cup tamari
2 tablespoons orange juice
½ pound daikon radish, peeled and cut into 1-inch cubes

In a small bowl, whisk together the honey, tamari, and orange juice until well blended; set aside.

In a food processor, use the pulse function to roughly puree half of the daikon cubes into the consistency of thick applesauce. Pour into a fine-mesh strainer (or a regular strainer lined with a coffee filter) to remove excess water. Add to the honey mixture. Repeat with the remaining daikon cubes. Mix thoroughly, then spoon into individual dipping bowls.

> *Note: This sauce is also an excellent condiment for grilled fish, such as Norwegian mackerel.*

Thai Memories Macadamia Nut Dressing & Toss Sauce

One year, Mom and I had a once-in-a-lifetime mother-daughter visit to Bangkok. Wanting to see the non-tourist side of the city and get away from the urban congestion, we stayed in a small bed-and-breakfast oasis that served vegetarian meals, and we signed up for a behind-the-scenes urban bicycle tour. The adept local guide led us through narrow back alleys, and we literally pedaled through the living spaces and kitchens of local residents with greetings of "Hello, hello!" as we trundled by. On one stretch, we had to navigate over a precarious three-foot-wide pathway over a rice paddy. Despite an incredible sunset view, we focused all our attention (and balance) on not falling off into the swampy water. The ingredients and aromas in this recipe take me back to this wonderful adventure in Southeast Asia with my favorite travel companion.

For an amazing twist on a turkey club sandwich, or with leftover holiday turkey, toss a package of slaw or salad greens in this dressing, and sprinkle in the unused Thai basil leaves (½ cup, roughly chopped).

In a blender on high speed, blend the nuts, peanut oil, peanut powder, cider, sugar, ginger, garlic, sesame oil, soy sauce, rice vinegar, apple cider vinegar, basil stems, fish sauce (if using), chile (if using), and salt to taste until smooth and emulsified.

Add the coconut water, 1 tablespoon at a time, until the desired consistency is reached (thicker for noodle sauce, thinner for salad dressing).

Serves 4 (2 to 4 tablespoons each)

½ cup macadamia nuts or
  ¼ cup almond butter
2 tablespoons peanut
  oil or pecan oil
¼ cup peanut powder
2 tablespoons fruit cider,
  preferably local
1 tablespoon turbinado
  cane sugar
1 ½ teaspoons grated ginger
2 garlic cloves, minced
1 tablespoon roasted sesame oil
¼ cup naturally brewed
  soy sauce
1 tablespoon rice vinegar
1 tablespoon apple cider vinegar
1 teaspoon chopped Thai basil
  stems (tender portion)
½ teaspoon fish sauce or
  anchovy brine (optional)
½ teaspoon finely minced
  red chile (optional)
Sea salt
½ cup coconut water
  or plain water

Night Market Cracked Peppercorn Steak Gravy

On my travels to Taiwan, one of the places that I look forward to most is the Shilin Night Market, or any of Taipei's bustling urban night markets. These markets have become must-see destinations on many a tour guide's list. Despite its humble origins as a condiment used in night market food stalls, nowadays Asian chefs from Tokyo to Taipei swear by this gravy-like steak sauce. Crack hack: To crack peppercorns without a grinder, put them on a cutting board and, with a heavy-bottomed saucepan, firmly press down while scooting the bottom of the pan across the top of the peppercorns.

In a medium, heat-resistant bowl, dissolve the bouillon in the hot water. Gently whisk in the half-and-half, mayonnaise, vinegar, and soy sauce and set aside.

In a 2-quart saucepan over medium heat, melt the butter. Add the shallots and cook for about 3 minutes, until softened. Add the garlic and ground peppercorns, then stir for about 30 seconds. Pour in the moonshine and increase the heat to medium-high. Cook for about 1 minute to reduce the liquid.

Reduce the heat to low and pour in the half-and-half mixture, mixing quickly to prevent burning. Simmer for about 5 minutes, stirring occasionally, until the sauce is thickened to a gravy consistency.

Serve the steak sauce in individual gravy boats to ladle over chicken-fried steak or pork chops, and make extra if serving on grilled burgers because guests will definitely want seconds!

Makes about 2 cups

- 3 ½ teaspoons Better Than Bouillon Roasted Beef Base
- 2 tablespoons plus 1 teaspoon hot water
- 1 ⅓ cups half-and-half
- 4 tablespoons reduced-fat mayonnaise
- 1 tablespoon dark rice vinegar
- 1 teaspoon premium dark naturally brewed soy sauce
- 2 tablespoons unsalted butter
- 2 shallots, finely chopped
- 2 garlic cloves, finely chopped
- 2 tablespoons ground black peppercorns
- ¼ cup Southern Secret Muscadine Moonshine, or moonshine of choice

Creamy Chili Crisp Aioli

When I first became involved in the NCCJ, it was still growing into its new moniker: The National Conference for Community and Justice. Prior to that, its name was the National Conference of Christians and Jews for the Advancement of Justice, Amity, and Peace. It made me wonder: What's in a name? When there is divisiveness and hatred, then every word matters. When there is justice, amity, and peace, the spirit of humanity and compassion override precision.

In the classic sense, aioli is derived from the Catalan word *allioli*, meaning "garlic and oil." However, my rendition of aioli omits the traditional garlic and, instead, merges the spicy, oniony elan of Sichuan chili sauce with the mellow nuttiness of sesame oil—a nod to Myanmar, the world's largest producer of sesame seeds. It goes great with Pan-Grilled Rice Bun Sliders with Salmon (page 141) or as a dip for vegetables, and it redefines burgers and baked potatoes. This simple, fun recipe goes to show, bucking tradition might raise eyebrows among the Kitchen Gods, but that doesn't stop folks from dipping and spreading it on everything.

Makes about ⅔ cup

½ cup Kewpie mayonnaise (see Resource Guide, page 9)

2 tablespoons spicy chili crisp or chili crunch

2 tablespoons roasted sesame oil

1 tablespoon naturally brewed soy sauce

1 tablespoon Homemade Sweet Chili Peach Dressing, page 161

¼ teaspoon salt

In a medium bowl, whisk together the mayonnaise, chili crisp, sesame oil, soy sauce, chili peach dressing, and salt until well combined.

Rebel Asian Pesto

This pesto recipe was inspired by my eye-opening "rebel years" as a college student when I took women's studies courses and attended the Women's March on Washington. There are countless types of pesto available—with or without cilantro, nuts, and green chiles. Thai basil adds anise- or licorice-like notes, while Italian basil is sweet and peppery. Create your own adaptation according to taste; that's the fun part.

If you don't have garlic scapes, add 1 to 2 extra cloves of garlic, increase the chopped green onions to ½ cup, and increase the chopped parsley to 1 cup.

In a food processor, puree the garlic, garlic scapes, green onions, oil, ginger, lemon juice, salt, and pepper to taste until smooth. In ½-cup batches, add the basil, parsley, and cilantro and blend until smooth. If the blender gets stuck, stir the paste gently with a spatula to loosen, and scrape down the sides in between batches. Don't overmix. Add the nuts (if using) and blend until smooth. Check the taste for seasonings. Add more salt, pepper, or lemon juice, if desired.

Store excess pesto in a lidded jar, and add a thin coating of olive oil. Refrigerate and eat within 1 week. If you make extra or want to store it longer, freeze the pesto in ice cube trays first, pop out the frozen cubes, and store the extra cubes in your freezer.

Note: This sauce is great served with hot pasta, mixed with sour cream and softened cream cheese for a sandwich spread, or stirred into a chicken salad.

Makes about 2 cups

4 garlic cloves, peeled

½ cup 1-inch pieces garlic scapes

¼ cup chopped green onions

1 cup olive oil

2 tablespoons grated fresh ginger

1 tablespoon lemon juice

½ tablespoon salt

Freshly ground black pepper

1 cup stemmed fresh Thai or Italian basil leaves

½ cup chopped parsley

½ cup chopped cilantro

¼ cup roasted peanuts or pine nuts (optional)

Hot Hot Hunan Fresh Chile Sambal

The phrase "You can't be a revolutionary if you don't eat chiles" is credited to Chairman Mao Zedong, who hailed from the province of Hunan. My gong-gong (maternal grandpa) was from Hunan. *Hunan* translates to "Lake South" and is a region known for its dry heat (or *red hot*, as we Southerners might put it). Regardless of what my po-po cooked and set in front of him, there had to be hot chiles—in it, on it, or with it. This sauce suits all three of those purposes. Gong-Gong always said, "One-minute garlic tastes better than ten-minute garlic," and the sequenced steps in this recipe are intended to capture the just-cut flavors of freshly minced aromatics.

To make the chile base, put the chopped chiles in a glass bowl and pour the vinegar over the chiles. Add the garlic and stir gently with chopsticks to coat and blend. Be careful not to break apart the chile pieces. Set aside.

In a 4-cup glass measuring cup, make the citrus mixture by combining the lemon juice, lime juice, and ginger. Set aside.

In a separate small bowl, make the cider mixture by stirring the honey into the fish sauce until dissolved, then add the cider and stir to combine.

Pour the cider mixture into the citrus mixture, stirring to combine.

Carefully pour or spoon the chile base into the glass measuring cup. Use chopsticks to gently combine all the sambal ingredients, then transfer to a serving bowl. If not serving the whole batch right away, spoon out the desired amount of chiles, add some of the cider-citrus liquid, and refrigerate the remaining sambal mixture in a mason jar for up to 3 weeks.

Makes about 1 cup

½ cup chopped fresh chiles (about 3 large cayenne or Anaheim chiles)

3 tablespoons light rice vinegar

6 garlic cloves, minced

Juice of 1 lemon (about 2 tablespoons)

Juice of 1 lime (about 2 tablespoons)

5 peeled ginger slices (⅛ inch thick and 1 inch in diameter)

½ teaspoon honey

½ teaspoon fish sauce

3 tablespoons muscadine cider

I-Lava-You Island Chunky BBQ Sauce with Pineapple & Coconut Sugar

The combination of coconut and pineapple conjures visions of Hawaii, where the U.S. pineapple industry flourished throughout the twentieth century. Ketchup is arguably America's most famous sauce, but while hoisin is a leading lady in Cantonese cooking, little is known about its origin and why its Mandarin name is "seafood sauce" when it contains no seafood. This lip-smackin' sauce pays tribute to the taste buds of explorers, travelers, and chefs whose myriad taste experiences and sense of entrepreneurship culminate in an explosion of flavors and ingredients from far-off regions of the world brought home to become iconic local condiments, like barbecue sauce.

In a 3-quart saucepan over medium-low heat, bring the shallot, ginger, and rice wine to a simmer. Cook for 8 to 10 minutes, until the shallot is translucent. Increase the heat to medium and add the cola, black pepper, white peppers, salt, ketchup, apple cider vinegar, dark rice vinegar, sugar, hoisin sauce, pineapple with its juices, and sriracha (if using), continuing to stir to combine. Bring the mixture to a boil, then reduce the heat to low and simmer for 20 minutes, taking care to stir occasionally as the sauce thickens and develops.

Remove from the heat and, if a smooth sauce is desired, puree in a blender. I like it chunky.

The sauce is ready to use immediately; or, allow it to cool for 10 minutes, then transfer to a heatproof, airtight container (such as a mason jar) and refrigerate for up to 2 weeks.

Makes about 2 ½ cups

1 shallot, minced (about ⅓ cup)
2 tablespoons finely minced ginger
½ cup Hong Biou Michiu quality-controlled Taiwan rice wine (21 percent alcohol) or cooking sherry
¼ cup Coca-Cola
½ teaspoon freshly ground black pepper
¼ teaspoon white pepper
½ teaspoon Hawaiian Alaea salt or sea salt
1 cup ketchup
⅓ cup apple cider vinegar
¼ cup dark rice vinegar or Worcestershire sauce
½ cup coconut sugar or dark brown sugar
¼ cup hoisin sauce or tomato paste
½ cup pineapple, chopped with juice (or canned, crushed)
½ teaspoon sriracha (optional)

Hawaiian Mango Sauce

There's nothing as tasty as a sweet-and-sour sauce made from scratch. This sauce was inspired by the homemade duck sauce served in our family restaurants. I use mango for a tropical twist or local peaches and honey (instead of brown sugar) for a Southern flair. Add a shake of hot sauce to kick it up. It's delicious as a dipping sauce for chicken or fish nuggets.

In a medium saucepan over medium heat, combine the orange juice, lemon juice, brown sugar, ginger sauce, salt, and cornstarch. Cook until bubbly and thickened. Gently stir in the mango and serve.

Makes about 2 cups

1 cup orange juice
2 tablespoons lemon juice
1/2 cup brown sugar
2 tablespoons Homemade Soy-Ginger Sauce (page 164)
1 teaspoon salt
1 tablespoon cornstarch
2 cups mangoes diced, fresh or canned

Homemade Sweet Chili Peach Dressing

This dressing was the inspiration for my award-winning My Sweet Hottie Sauce available in stores. This version is a light, naturally zesty sweet-and-tangy blend that features fresh local peaches and tomatoes when in season. It brightens up salads and slaw (such as Sweet Chili Peach Napa Slaw, page 103) and works well as a marinade for fish and shrimp.

In a medium bowl, stir together the garlic, ginger, pepper jelly, honey, peach puree, tomato paste, vinegar, salt, and hot sauce (if using). Slowly drizzle the avocado oil then the sesame oil into the bowl while vigorously whisking the dressing mixture to emulsify.

Use immediately or transfer to a covered container and refrigerate for later use. Whisk again before use if the oil and vinegar separate.

Makes about 1/2 cup

1 garlic clove, crushed
1 teaspoon grated ginger
1 teaspoon jalapeño pepper jelly
2 tablespoons local honey
1 tablespoon peach puree
1 1/2 teaspoons tomato paste
1/3 cup seasoned rice vinegar
1/2 teaspoon salt
1/2 teaspoon sriracha (optional)
1 tablespoon avocado oil or olive oil
1 tablespoon toasted sesame oil

Sesame Sammie Spread & Veggie Dip

This dip is a great way to get kids to eat more vegetables, and it is so good with slices of apple and/or banana on multigrain bread. For sandwiches, toast bread and prepare fruit slices, then spread and assemble. Celery is a throwback to after-school celery boats, and the crunchiness of celery is inimitably satisfying. This is also good on crackers.

In a small bowl, combine the peanut butter, sesame oil, olive oil, mirin, honey, soy sauce, balsamic vinegar, and apple cider vinegar, then stir vigorously with a fork until smooth and blended. To make the spread thinner, add more olive or vegetable oil. To thicken, add more peanut butter. Do not add water because the peanut butter mixture will not emulsify properly.

Makes ½ cup

4 tablespoons natural Georgia Grinders Creamy Peanut Butter or peanut butter of choice

2 teaspoons roasted sesame oil

2 teaspoons extra virgin olive oil

2 teaspoons mirin

2 teaspoons honey

2 teaspoons naturally brewed light soy sauce

½ teaspoon balsamic vinegar

½ teaspoon apple cider vinegar

Homemade
Soy-Ginger Sauce

Our motto is "Have ginger, will cook." This classic and versatile base sauce from our mother-daughter kitchen is for all things tossed, marinated, and drizzled. Savory and more complex in flavor than plain soy sauce or sugary hoisin, this sauce emulates the essence of my award-winning sauce, You Saucy Thing Marinade, Stir-Fry & Braising Sauce, which was inspired by my love of fresh garden vegetables and my three wishes as a home cook: fast, fresh, and yummy.

In a small saucepan over medium-low heat, dissolve the cornstarch in 2 tablespoons of water, then add the remaining water, soy sauce, ginger, garlic, sugar, wine, vinegar, and sesame oil. Whisk together until the sugar and cornstarch are completely dissolved, and bring to a boil while stirring frequently for 3 to 4 minutes, until the sauce thickens and is shiny and translucent.

To use as a cooking sauce, pour over the prepared meat, fish, or vegetables. To use as a dipping sauce, allow to cool for 10 minutes.

Makes about 1 cup

1 tablespoon cornstarch

½ cup water, divided

½ cup naturally brewed soy sauce

1 teaspoon grated ginger or ginger paste

1 teaspoon minced garlic

2 tablespoons sugar

1 tablespoon Hong Biou Michiu quality-controlled Taiwan rice wine or cooking wine

1 tablespoon rice vinegar

½ teaspoon roasted sesame oil

Homemade Teriyaki Sauce

I was a skinny little kid. Despite being an athlete and rarely getting sick, my grandparents were worried about my health and piled extra rice and meat on my plate. Instead of "mangia, mangia!" in Italian, it was "ch-er, ch-er!" in Mandarin. They insisted Mom take me to the doctor "in case I had tapeworms." One day in high school, I finally surpassed my petite grandmother in height (all of 4 feet 8 inches). It was a huge milestone celebrated with a big plate of Grandma's Teriyaki Pork Chops (page 131) made with this sauce, and ice cream pie for dessert. This is a homemade version of my Wild Wild East Asian BBQ & Teriyaki Pineapple sauce, a crowd pleaser and hands-down kid favorite.

Makes about 1 cup

1 tablespoon cornstarch

1 cup water, divided

¼ cup naturally brewed soy sauce

3 tablespoons brown sugar

1 tablespoon molasses or honey

1 teaspoon pineapple puree

1 garlic clove, finely minced

½ teaspoon grated ginger

In a small saucepan over medium-low heat, dissolve the cornstarch in 2 tablespoons of water, then add the remaining water, soy sauce, brown sugar, molasses, pineapple puree, garlic, and ginger. Whisk together until the sugar and cornstarch are completely dissolved. Bring to a boil while stirring frequently for 3 to 4 minutes, until the sauce thickens and is shiny and translucent.

To use as a cooking sauce, pour over the prepared meat, fish, or vegetables. To use as a dipping sauce, allow to cool for 10 minutes.

Semisweets

Growing up, *dessert* in our household meant fruit, like a slice of watermelon or when guests were over, a bowl of special fruit like lychee and fruit cocktail. Whether no real desserts were perceived as a horrible childhood deprivation or a blessing in disguise, truth be told, our taste buds led the way. I didn't like anything sweeter than a fried peach pie or a dipped cone from the neighborhood Dairy Queen.

Georgia is famous for its beautiful colonial-style homes. I remember my father taking our whole family on a driving tour every year, just after the third week in December. "Let's go see the Christmas lights on West Paces Ferry (Road)" had a dual meaning for me. One, it meant my Christmas birthday was nearing. Two, it meant Santa was probably packing up his sleigh. I remember being mesmerized by the exquisitely decorated lawns. My dad would drive as slowly as he could, and we would, *Pray that no one would drive up behind us. Whoa. Look at that mansion.* My mom adores Christmas lights. Her jewelry-making station is adorned with a curtain of colorful beads, many of which my dad found for her at his favorite lollygagging spot: antique shows. "They remind me of Christmas lights," she told me. Now, every year, we drive down to Callaway Gardens for the Fantasy in Lights. Lychee Fruit Cocktail with Almond Gelatin (page 172) harkens back to the decorated, sometimes snow-covered lawns of our holiday drives, and the shiny little Candied Tomato Bites (page 181), with their glassy finish, are reminiscent of Mom's beads and the love with which she stranded them into gifts for us.

When a friend's apiary in rural Georgia was going under, I ordered all of their stock (sixty pounds!) of honey, much of it gallberry, to give them one last injection of cash. Gallberry bushes grow along the swamps and piney woods of southern Georgia and northern Florida, producing a delicious native American honey that has become a favored varietal throughout Europe. This is how I came to use gallberry honey in sweets recipes.

For Dad's Sweet Peanut Soup (page 183), any peanuts will do, but Southern peanuts are the best. Do you know that half the peanuts grown in the United States are farmed within a hundred-mile radius of Dothan, Alabama? But what is most special about my sweet peanut soup is not the dish itself. For me, this recipe embodies the theme of this book. On one hand, it is the American Dream in a bowl—a heritage family recipe created by a first-gen immigrant who (literally) came over on a boat, yet he used all Southern ingredients to cook up his show-off dish. On the other hand, my family's sweet peanut soup, which originated as a blip in my inbox as a father-daughter recipe from a dad who types using his pointer fingers, stands as the perfect example of how cultural comfort foods encapsulate intergenerational love, a language that transcends the country on your birth certificate, your passport, and your home address—even if all three are different.

Father & Son—Yeh-Yeh, the revered Army General who, after seeing the ravages of war, swore off the trappings of modernity and ate a stew of Spam with garden vegetables for the rest of his life, pictured with his son (my dad), the NASA rocket engineer.

Gotcha Matcha Ice Cream Pie

As a child I had a dairy allergy and couldn't eat ice cream. Mom prohibited my sisters from eating ice cream in front of me to prevent meltdowns. They hid behind the sofa to eat their ice cream, but I still caught them. In Taiwan, dairy farms were scarce and full-fat cream was an imported luxury, so kids there grow up eating shaved ice with toppings such as sweetened adzuki beans and lotus seeds. With this dessert, you can have your pie and eat it, too! Matcha tea is believed to have health benefits, such as disease-thwarting antioxidants and metabolism-boosting polyphenols.

Serves 6

½ gallon vanilla ice cream

2 tablespoons matcha green tea powder

⅛ teaspoon almond extract

1 (10-inch) prepared graham cracker piecrust

¼ cup sliced almonds, for garnishing

Whipped cream, for garnishing

Thaw the ice cream until it is slightly soft, then scoop it out into a large mixing bowl. Add the matcha powder and almond extract. With a large metal spoon or sturdy wooden spoon, blend well into the ice cream until it is an even shade of matcha green, about 2 minutes of mixing. Don't let the ice cream melt into a liquid. Fill the entire piecrust with an even layer of the ice cream mixture. Put the pie in the freezer to firm up, about 1 hour. Slice and serve the ice cream pie garnished with almonds and whipped cream.

Black Sesame & Almond Mini Croissants

This recipe was inspired by my first trip to Paris, which was with my high-school French class. We were supposed to be practicing our French, but all I noticed were the boys pointing to me and exclaiming excitedly, "Chinoise, chinoise, belle!" It was the first time I had experienced any flirting. It was a nice compliment and a welcome change. These little treats disappear so fast that I keep a roll of crescent dough in the fridge and premake a double batch of the filling recipe to freeze. It can be easily assembled as a quick after-school snack, potluck dish, or brunch pastry.

Makes 8 croissants

Vegetable oil, for greasing
$\frac{1}{2}$ cup black sesame powder
$\frac{1}{4}$ cup powdered milk
  (whole or nonfat)
3 tablespoons sugar
$\frac{1}{4}$ teaspoon almond extract
$\frac{1}{2}$ cup hot water, divided
1 (8-count) can regular size
  refrigerated crescent rolls
Toasted black or white
  sesame seeds

Preheat the oven to 350°F. Lightly grease or spray a baking sheet with vegetable oil.

In a medium bowl, mix the sesame powder, powdered milk, sugar, and almond extract with 3 tablespoons of hot water. Stir for about 30 seconds, or until the sugar is thoroughly dissolved. Let the mixture sit for 1 minute. The paste will thicken up a bit. Check the consistency—if it's too dry or thick, it will be hard to spread on the soft dough. Repeat the process with 1 teaspoon of water at a time until the paste is spreadable and smooth.

Separate the dough into 8 triangles. Spread about 1 tablespoon of the sesame paste in a thin, even layer across each triangle. Starting at the shortest side of the triangle, gently roll up the dough covered in paste to the opposite point. Place on the prepared baking sheet 2 inches apart and sprinkle the top of each croissant with a touch of sesame seeds. Press the seeds gently into the dough to make sure they stick. Bake for 12 to 14 minutes, or until golden brown. Serve immediately.

Zesty Ginger-Peach Cobbler

In our home, dessert was fruit. Despite two peach trees in our yard, Mom didn't bake (she used the oven to store pots and pans). I learned to bake just so I could make this traditional Georgia treat. Turbinado sugar is less processed and imparts a subtle sweetness that lets the natural fruitiness of local, ripe peaches shine through. This recipe purposely doesn't require cooking or peeling the peaches and tastes wonderful even if they don't soften completely during baking. Also, the sugar quantity is reduced, because I like being able to eat as much as I want without worrying about a sugar crash!

Preheat the oven to 350°F.

In a large bowl, combine the peaches with ½ cup of the sugar, the ginger, and the cayenne and let stand for 10 minutes. Melt the butter in an 8 x 12-inch baking dish and set aside.

In a medium bowl, combine the whole wheat flour, all-purpose flour, remaining ½ cup of sugar, baking powder, and salt. Add the milk and mix well. Pour the batter into the prepared baking dish. Pour the peach mixture evenly over the batter (do not stir). Bake for 50 minutes, or until the top is golden brown.

Serve warm with vanilla ice cream and a sprinkle of orange-chile sugar.

Serves 5

4 cups sliced peaches

1 cup turbinado sugar, divided

2 teaspoons finely grated ginger

¼ teaspoon cayenne pepper

½ cup butter

½ cup whole wheat flour

½ cup all-purpose flour

1 ½ teaspoons baking powder

½ teaspoon salt

¾ cup milk

Vanilla ice cream, for serving

Orange-chile sugar, for sprinkling (I like Beautiful Briny Sea's version)

Lychee Fruit Cocktail with Almond Gelatin

As a youngster, I looked forward to this light, refreshing treat at the end of a long wedding dinner or Lunar New Year's banquet. It was a special dish that was symbolic of luck and prosperity, but I was just thrilled to have a gelatin dessert! No matter how many courses of food there were, I always had room for this dessert. I loved the taste and look of the solid white blocks jiggling with the bright colors of peaches, oranges, and cherries. This is a healthy, easy, not-so-sweet dessert that will make the whole family smile.

Serves 6

2 (0.25-ounce) packets
    unflavored gelatin
2 cups boiling water
½ cup sugar
1 ½ cups whole milk
1 tablespoon pure almond
    extract, plus more to taste
1 (15.25-ounce) can fruit
    cocktail with syrup
½ cup lychee fruit, fresh or
    canned, peeled and diced
½ cup diced mango (optional)

In a medium bowl, mix and dissolve the gelatin completely in the boiling water, about 3 minutes. Mix in the sugar until dissolved. Stir in the milk and almond extract. Pour the gelatin mixture into an 8 x 8 or similar rectangular baking dish and refrigerate about 2 hours or until completely set. When it has set, cut the gelatin into 1-inch cubes.

In a large bowl, mix the gelatin cubes and the fruit cocktail with the syrup, lychee, and mango (if using) together. Add a few more drops of almond extract, if desired. Serve chilled in small dessert cups.

Vanilla Rice Pudding with Black-Eyed Peas & Coconut Milk Topping

Peas and beans in a dessert recipe may seem like an odd pairing to those unfamiliar with traditional sweet bean pastes and pastries. Add black-eyed peas to the sweet mix, and a culinary explanation is reasonably in order. Visit a Vietnamese market and you'll likely see a refrigerator full of clear plastic cups filled with rice, milk, fresh tropical fruit bits, tapioca balls, adzuki beans, mung beans—and black-eyed peas! I love red adzuki bean ice milk desserts. It's like a semisweet dessert snack in a bowl!

To make the pudding: Fill a medium saucepan halfway with water and bring to a boil. Add the black-eyed peas and blanch for 10 seconds. Drain the peas and transfer to a small bowl. Sprinkle 2 tablespoons of sugar into the peas, toss, and set aside.

In a large saucepan over high heat, bring the 3 ¾ cups of water to a boil. While the water is heating, rinse the rice until the water runs clear. Add the rice to the boiling water and stir. Reduce the heat to medium-low and cover the pot loosely so steam can still escape. Cook the rice for 15 to 20 minutes, stirring occasionally to prevent the rice from clumping.

In a small bowl, whisk together the tapioca starch and the remaining 2 tablespoons of water. Set aside. Add the peas to the pot of rice and stir together. Add the remaining 8 tablespoons of sugar to the pot and mix well.

Stir the tapioca starch and water mixture again, then pour into the pudding along with the vanilla extract. Stir well. Simmer on low heat for another 5 minutes, or until the mixture thickens.

Serves 4

FOR THE RICE PUDDING
1 (15-ounce) can black-eyed peas, drained and well rinsed
½ cup sugar, divided
3 ¾ cups plus 2 tablespoons water, divided
¾ cup uncooked white or black glutinous rice (also called sweet rice)
1 ½ tablespoons tapioca starch or ½ tablespoon cornstarch
¼ teaspoon vanilla extract

FOR THE COCONUT MILK TOPPING
1 (5.6-ounce) can coconut milk
½ cup water
1 tablespoon sugar
⅛ teaspoon salt
1 tablespoon tapioca starch or ½ tablespoon cornstarch
Fresh mango or peach slices (optional)

To make the coconut milk topping: In a small saucepan, whisk together the coconut milk, water, sugar, salt, and tapioca starch until well blended.

Over medium heat, cook the coconut milk mixture, stirring constantly until it starts to thicken, 2 to 3 minutes. Remove from the heat.

To serve, spoon the rice pudding into dessert bowls, drizzle on the coconut milk mixture, and top with mango or peach slices (if using). Enjoy hot or cold. Store leftover pudding and coconut milk in the refrigerator for up to 1 week.

Sweet Rice Balls & Bols with Pear

I prefer the poetic Mandarin name *tang yuan* to the English "sticky rice balls." Whatever you might call them, these soft, plump little bubbles with a rich, sweet black-sesame butter filling are packed with protein, fiber, and iron encased in gooey, chewy, sweet rice. Any brand of frozen glutinous rice balls with a sweet filling will work for this dish. Laurel's uses pure locally grown glutinous rice from Taiwan's Zhuoshui River, making it a premium choice. For a non-alcoholic version, replace the Curaçao with a drizzle of honey.

Serves 5

2 pears
½ cup plus 2 tablespoons
   Bols Blue Curaçao
1 (10-count) package frozen
   Laurel's Sesame Rice Balls

Fill a 2-quart saucepan with water and bring to a boil. Wash, core, and cut the pears into bite-size chunks, then set aside. Pour 2 tablespoons of Curaçao into each of 5 serving bowls and set aside.

Using a slotted spoon, carefully place the frozen rice balls in the boiling water. With a pair of chopsticks, slowly swirl the water around to prevent the balls from sticking to the bottom of the pot. Return to a boil, then reduce the heat to low. Gently swirl the water again and wait for the balls to float to the surface. Continue cooking for another 5 to 8 minutes, until the balls are soft and pliable.

In the final minutes of cooking, ladle ¼ cup hot water from the pot and 4 or 5 pieces of pear into each bowl. Place 2 balls in each bowl with the pears.

Serve with a Chinese soup spoon.

Ginger-Honey Pears

"Don't judge a fruit by its peel," Grandpa always said. He meant it literally: Don't throw out the fruit or vegetable just because it has brown spots, insect holes, or blemishes on the outside. Before organic certification standards, Grandpa's standards ruled the roost. "Pick the apples with insect holes. No chemicals." So I always keep this in mind when choosing fruit to make fresh fruit snacks and desserts like these honeyed, gingery pears. I also try to tie in local ingredients whenever possible.

Serves 4

¼ cup turbinado sugar
1 tablespoon honey
1 cup water
2 giant Asian pears or
    4 Anjou or Bosc pears,
    cored, peeled, and halved
1 tablespoon minced ginger
Five-spice seasoning (optional)

In a small pot over low heat, dissolve the sugar and honey in the water. Add the pears and ginger and simmer for 12 to 15 minutes. Transfer the pears to dessert bowls and serve with a pinch of five-spice seasoning (if using).

I like to let the syrup reduce for another 5 to 10 minutes and serve it over the pears or with ice cream.

Black Sesame Cupcakes with Matcha Frosting

With this nutty-but-not-too-sweet cupcake, I salute my predecessor, Amelia Simmons, author of our nation's first known cookbook, titled in full: *American Cookery, or the Art of Dressing Viands, Fish, Poultry, and Vegetables, and the Best Modes of Making Pastes, Puffs, Pies, Tarts, Puddings, Custards, and Preserves, and All Kinds of Cakes, from the Imperial Plum to Plain Cake: Adapted to This Country, and All Grades of Life.* Among the "all kinds of cakes" was a recipe for "a light Cake to bake in small cups" that is widely acknowledged as the first cupcake. *American Cookery*, as the book is now known, was published in 1796. I hope that 220-odd years from now, someone will still be enjoying the wonderfully worldly homestyle recipes that my generation has adapted "to this country, and all grades of life."

To make the cupcakes: Preheat the oven to 350°F. Line 12 standard muffin cups with paper liners.

In a medium bowl, combine the sesame powder, flour, almond powder, cocoa powder, baking powder, and salt. In a large bowl, use an electric mixer to beat the butter, tahini, and brown sugar 1 minute, until pale and creamy. Add the eggs 1 at a time, beating well after each addition. Pour in the vanilla. Add the flour mixture and beat on low speed to combine, then blend in the milk. Scoop the batter into the muffin cups, filling each about ⅔ full.

Bake 15 to 18 minutes, until the cupcakes have slightly risen, the tops are lightly golden, and a toothpick inserted into the center comes out clean. Let the cupcakes cool for a few minutes in the pan, then transfer them to a wire rack to cool completely.

Serves 12

FOR THE BLACK SESAME CUPCAKES

⅓ cup roasted black sesame powder

1 ¼ cups all-purpose flour

1 tablespoon almond powder

1 teaspoon cocoa powder

1 teaspoon baking powder

½ teaspoon salt

½ cup unsalted butter, room temperature

¼ cup tahini

¾ cup brown sugar

2 large eggs

2 teaspoons vanilla extract

⅔ cup milk

To make the frosting: In a medium bowl, use an electric mixer to beat together the butter, powdered sugar, matcha, and vanilla until creamy and spreadable. Taste and add more sugar or matcha, to taste. Using a small spatula or spoon, spread the frosting on top of the cooled cupcakes. I only like a light layer so it's not too sweet.

FOR THE MATCHA FROSTING

1 cup butter, room temperature

1 ½ cups powdered sugar

1 ½ teaspoons matcha
   green tea powder

½ teaspoon vanilla extract

Note: For an easy, homemade frosting dispenser, scoop all of the icing into a quart-size plastic storage or sandwich bag. Gently press and gather the frosting toward one corner of the bag. Snip off the very tip of the plastic bag, creating a small hole. Gently squeeze the frosting out of the hole onto the cupcakes in a pretty design.

Candied Tomato Bites

"Fruit is dessert," Mom asserted as she served us a plate of sliced watermelon after dinner. What could be better than a candied dessert? These little gems are almost too pretty to eat. Be ready to swirl these at a brisk pace when cooking. Don't worry if it's not a perfect coating—the imperfects taste the same as the perfects, and sometimes I intentionally coat just half the tomato so it's not so sweet. Any remaining syrup can be enjoyed as hard candy. The swirl-coating technique takes a bit of practice, but the result, perfect or not, will be pretty as a picture once you get the hang of it.

Makes 15 to 20 candied tomatoes

15 to 20 cherry tomatoes (about 3/4 pint), washed and thoroughly dried
Cooking oil, for greasing
3/4 cup water
2/3 cup organic light corn syrup
2 cups sugar
A small bowl of water with ice (for testing hardness)

Skewer each tomato with a toothpick or wooden sandwich skewer and set near the stovetop. Lightly grease a large baking sheet with oil or use a silicone mat. Keep the prepared baking sheet as close to the stovetop as possible during the dipping process.

In a heavy-bottomed 2-quart saucepan, combine the water, corn syrup, and sugar and mix well. Over medium heat (medium-high if experienced in candy making), bring the mixture to a full boil (212°F using a candy thermometer). This may take 5 minutes, possibly longer. Once boiling, do not stir any more. Using a wet silicone pastry brush, wash down any sugar crystals that form on the sides of the pan. This will help prevent crystallization. Be extra careful when working with hot sugar and don't leave the pot unattended.

Set a timer for 7 minutes and continue to cook the syrup, without stirring, until the temperature reaches 300°F. This may take 10 to 15 minutes in total, possibly longer. Unless experienced, do not turn up the heat. (Patience will be rewarded as longer cooking times rarely end up problematic.) At the 7-minute timer, use a chopstick to drizzle a bit of syrup into the ice water to check the hardness. The sugar should still be pliable. As soon as the mixture reaches 300°F (generally another 3 to 4 minutes, but could be longer), do another test to confirm that the hard-crack stage has been reached. Hard-crack stage is technically at 310°F, but 300°F is usually enough and will allow more time for coating. At hard-crack stage, the syrup forms threadlike strands when dropped into ice water, and it is crispy to bite. Turn the heat down to medium-low and begin the coating process. Rookies might need to turn the heat off, coat some, then reheat the syrup as needed.

continued

Working swiftly, swirl each skewered tomato by rotating it 360 degrees among the bubbles on the surface of the syrup, to coat the fruit without dunking the entire tomato into the syrup, which will result in a lollipop-like effect. Swirling the skewers at a horizontal diagonal and a flatter angle will help you coat the tomato in a quick motion. Ideally, you want a nice thin coat that results in a crisp outside that isn't too hard to bite. When the syrup level falls too low for dipping, you can use a metal spoon to spoon the syrup over the tomato. If the syrup mixture gets too hard during the dipping process, reheat it over medium heat and start swirling again.

The coating should glaze up and harden right away. Place each tomato on the prepared baking sheet as they are being made, so the bottoms form into flat surfaces and allow them to stand up. Then transfer them to a lightly oiled serving platter. Tomato bites are best enjoyed immediately. To take them to a party, allow them to cool, then promptly transfer to an airtight container to store either at room temperature or in the refrigerator.

Notes: Take caution, as melted sugar can result in one of the worst burns in the kitchen. This recipe should always be left to adults.

Typically, there are 25 to 30 cherry tomatoes in a pint. But I've found that a cushion is generally needed, for sampling and to account for defective fruit or insufficient time, as the window for swirl-coating is limited and may not allow for all the tomatoes to be coated. Just remember, buying a pint and having leftover tomatoes is fine.

You can make a hard candy with the leftover syrup. Oil a second baking sheet with about ½ teaspoon of oil. Working carefully, pour the excess hot syrup onto the prepared baking sheet. Let cool. Using the back of a cleaver or a rolling pin, break the hardened candy into pieces. Store in an airtight container for up to 3 days. Try melting bits and pieces in a hot cup of tea or coffee.

Dad's Sweet Peanut Soup

One chilly spring morning, my dad brought over some peanut soup that he had made. Lugged across town in a thermal pot, it was still hot when he arrived. While slurping up my second bowlful, I tried to get the recipe. He replied, "I made it up," and said he couldn't remember any of the details. I woke up the next morning to find this email in my inbox: "Cook raw peanuts (no shell) until they are very very soft, then add honey, brown sugar, and/or Smucker's Sweet Orange Marmalade. Love, Dad." There they were, the ingredients that had warmed my tummy and my heart—except for one. You'll need to add your own TLC.

Wash the peanuts, then soak them in a large bowl or pot of water, fully submerged, overnight.

When finished soaking, drain the peanuts and transfer them to an Instant Pot or similar pressure cooker. Fill the pot with enough filtered water to submerge the peanuts, with about $\frac{1}{2}$ inch overage at the top. Add the sugar and the marmalade. Stir briefly to distribute.

Using the Manual mode, set the pot to Low Pressure and cook for 30 minutes. When done, allow a natural release. Typically, this takes 20 to 30 minutes. Allowing longer, up to 1 hour without opening, will result in softer peanuts. When the floating valve pops down, shift the release valve to Venting and release the remaining pressure.

Carefully open the lid and drizzle in the honey. Stir gently to dissolve and taste for sweetness. I add the honey last, when the temperature is lower, as a way to preserve the healthful spectrum of enzymes in the honey, which help to prevent bloating from eating legumes. The soup can be served right away. Ladle into small dessert bowls. Change the setting to Slow Cook mode to keep warm for up to 2 hours. Refrigerate leftovers. This soup is also delicious when served chilled.

Serves: 4 to 5

1 pound blanched, shelled, skinless whole Alabama peanuts or peanuts of choice

2 tablespoons Florida Crystals Organic Light Brown Raw Cane Sugar or brown sugar of choice

1 tablespoon Georgia orange marmalade or orange marmalade of choice

$\frac{1}{4}$ cup Tupelo or gallberry honey

Teatime, Sips & Toddies

Tea, in its rudimentary form as an herb, fruit, or vegetable, steeped or cooked in water, is a common thread among world cultures. I prefer tea to coffee and have included several teas, both hot and cold, that conjure up good memories while embodying the essence and diversity of global "tea-ology." My dad is the genius behind Dad's Classic Sweet Iced Tea (page 199), the flagship thirst quencher from which this book project drew inspiration for its title. When he was working on heat transfer technology for NASA, the governor once served him iced tea, leaving him forever associating this beverage with Georgia's cream of the crop. Consequently, he spent countless hours developing the sweet tea that would accompany his best-in-class egg rolls, aiming to get it just the way Southerners—and the governor—liked it.

My rendition has only one tiny fusion tweak—the addition of a tea bag of high mountain oolong tea (for the six-serving recipe), to add a touch more complexity, for the indulgence of tea lovers like myself. I've also replaced white sugar with amber rock sugar (the kind made from cane sugar), which is coveted by the high-tea elite in England for having an ethereal way of sweetening connoisseur teas without altering the delicate flavor profile. That, and I used to suck on rock candy as a kid. We used to put lids on half-filled jars of sweet tea, label them using pieces of masking tape with our names written on them, and line them up inside the refrigerator-door shelf, next to the ketchup and soy sauce, ready to be filled with ice and guzzled down after playing in the sweltering Southern sun.

Top: The Georgia Tech campus was a second home. On his graduation day, my father captured this shot of his young family, enjoying a brunch of eggs, bacon, biscuits, and grits with a glass of sweet iced tea.

Middle: Scolded for playing too many sports, Dad hid his trophies under his bed, kept playing, aced the entrance exams, and attended a prestigious Presbyterian University.

Bottom: From being his favorite (and smallest) football wide receiver to being the first Asian American in my hometown to run for city council, my dad never let "being a girl" be a limitation to what I could do or achieve.

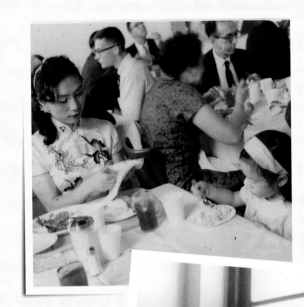

Jasmine & Honey Sweet Tea

This is a lovely, refreshing tea to serve for Sunday brunch, or a rebel tea deserving rebuke, depending on how you drink it. I once put some sugar and ice in my jasmine tea. It instigated a tsunami of gossip: Natalie puts sugar in her teh (Taiwanese for tea) and ice! Funny how a few grains of sugar and some frozen water could elicit such an uproar. I was on the receiving end of many talking-tos by elders, including metaphors like "It's the equivalent of adding Coke to a dram of coveted Black Tot!" (British Royal Naval Rum). Rare teas are auctioned like rare rums—among the most expensive teas in China is panda dung tea, which is grown in soil fertilized with panda bear droppings. I think I'll stick to jasmine. While any brand will do, I particularly like the aromatic balance of Just Add Honey Tea Company's loose blend of long leaf tips of green tea with rolled jasmine pearls. I still like it sweetened . . . but I've switched to honey.

Serves 1

1 cup water

1 teaspoon loose leaves jasmine green tea, or 1 tea bag

1 to 2 teaspoons sugar or honey

In a kettle or small saucepan over high heat, boil the water, then remove from the heat. Put the tea leaves in the teapot or a tea ball infuser. Add the just-boiled water and steep for 2 minutes.

Strain the tea leaves from the teapot and pour the hot tea into a cup. Add the sugar or honey and stir until dissolved. Enjoy hot or iced.

Cinnamon-Molasses Oolong Milk Tea

I drink tea year-round: hot, cold, iced, sweet iced tea (of course), and straight up. Like a fine wine or craft beer, fine tea has a wide range of subtle overtones and layers of aromas that make "tea-ology" a fun, fascinating hobby. This beverage highlights some of my favorite flavors: cinnamon, molasses, and vanilla. Oat milk, soy milk, almond milk, and cashew milk make delectable dairy-free variations. For a stress-relieving, tummy-warming afternoon pick-me-up, add a teaspoon of finely grated fair-trade, bean-to-bar chocolate!

Serves 2

2 cups water

3 cinnamon sticks

2 oolong tea bags

1 ½ cups milk of choice

3 teaspoons molasses syrup or maple syrup

1 teaspoon vanilla extract

In a small saucepan over high heat, bring the water and cinnamon sticks to a boil. Remove from the heat and add the tea bags. Cover the pan and let the tea bags steep for about 5 minutes.

In another small saucepan, heat the milk until it is steaming hot but not boiling. Remove from the heat and set aside. When the tea is ready, remove the tea bags from the pan. To avoid dripping tea bags, gently press the liquid out of each bag against the side wall of the pan with a spoon before discarding. Remove and discard the cinnamon sticks.

Stir the syrup and vanilla into the tea. Mix in the milk.

Share between 2 tea cups and serve hot.

Thai Mint-Iceberg Daiquiri

I discovered this drink when I made too many lettuce wraps for a party in the Georgia summer heat. I was tired, thirsty, and needed a pick-me-up, so I threw together the ingredients on hand with some water and ice in the blender! Later I changed the water to green tea and added rum to make it a cocktail, but it's totally delicious booze-free, too. Sweet, ripe honeydew melon is a tasty add-in.

In a blender, combine the tea, lettuce, honeydew, lime juice, honey, mint, basil, ginger, rum (if using), and ice and blend until you have a frozen daiquiri consistency. Add more ice if needed and extra honey to taste. Share between two glasses and garnish with lime slices.

Serves 2

2 cups brewed green tea

½ cup chopped iceberg lettuce

1 cup 1-inch chunks ripe
   honeydew melon

¼ cup lime juice

¼ cup honey, plus more

3 to 4 sprigs fresh mint leaves

3 to 4 sprigs fresh Thai
   sweet basil leaves

½ teaspoon grated fresh ginger

1 splash rum (optional)

Handful ice cubes

Lime slices, for garnishing

Moroccan-Style Wild Spearmint Sweet Iced Tea

Spearmint grew wild in our backyard. Neighbors complained that it grew too abundantly, choking out beloved jonquil flowers, and they mowed it down like weeds. But even now, despite its bounty, I never seem to have enough. When in season, I pick extra bunches to use in a variety of recipes from mint tea to Sweet Chili Peach Napa Slaw (page 103) to Smoked Salmon Summer Rolls (page 17). Extra cuttings can be carefully stemmed, dried, and stashed away for the winter. When abundant fresh leaves are on hand, I make this Moroccan-style minty and sweet herbal tea concentrate, sometimes with added green tea leaves. If using tea bags, I recommend steeping a couple mint and rich Indian Assam tea bags together. This recipe is for a sweet tea concentrate—so like the wild mint growing everywhere, feel free to adjust the strength and sweetness to your liking.

Makes 4 servings

4 cups water

2 handfuls fresh spearmint leaves, rinsed and stemmed, or 4 mint tea bags

½ cup amber rock sugar

2 tablespoons Tupelo or local clover honey

Ice cubes, for serving

4 to 6 sprigs of mint, for garnishing

Pour the water into a medium saucepan, cover, and bring it to a boil. While the water is heating, if using fresh mint leaves, muddle or tenderize the leaves using the back of a cleaver or mortar and pestle (mojito-style), releasing all the aromatic mint oils.

When the water reaches a full boil, turn off the heat and uncover. Allow the boiling water to aerate for 1 minute. This will help reduce any chlorine taste in the water. Replace the cover and bring to a full boil again. Remove the pot from the heat and put all the muddled mint leaves (or tea bags with strings and tags removed) in the pot of hot water. Using a wooden spoon, stir and press the leaves around for maximum flavor. Steep for 6 to 8 minutes. With a slotted spoon or spider strainer, remove the steeped leaves from the pot. (I don't bother straining out the little bits and pieces of fresh mint.) Add the honey. Pour the rock sugar into a large spoon or ladle, then lower it into the pot (to prevent splashing). Using a whisk or spoon, stir and dissolve the sugar and honey completely in the hot tea water. (If you prefer, you can add and mix the sugar in individual serving glasses for varying sweetness.) It will take a few minutes.

To serve, fill 4 (12-ounce) mason jars or glasses with ice cubes. Pour in the warm tea concentrate and stir. Top off with more ice and add sprigs of mint for garnish. Drink with eco-friendly bamboo or reusable straws, if you like. Of course, this can be sipped hot, too, like an afternoon or after-dinner dessert tea.

Golden Milk & Sorghum Hot Toddy

When I moved to Boston to attend Harvard University for graduate school, I experienced not only a change of food (no grits in the café!) and surroundings but also freezing weather and snow through April. Wool hats, mittens, and polar fleece sweaters became my best friends . . . along with hot beverages. Contrary to the "Asian whiz kid" stereotype, I had to study around the clock with late-night study-group sessions. Since I wasn't a regular coffee drinker, this haldi ka doodh–inspired, spiced turmeric milk toddy was the perfect beverage not only to keep me warm but also to soothe colds and sore throats and to kick-start my day or night, all without caffeine. This beverage is a warm, spicy substitute for a holiday toddy or a comfort beverage when you are feeling under the weather. The recipe can easily be adjusted to yield additional servings by doubling or tripling the ingredients.

Serves 1

¼ teaspoon ground turmeric
¼ teaspoon ground cardamom
⅛ teaspoon cocoa powder
1 pinch ground ginger
1 pinch ground cloves
1 pinch ground allspice
1 cup milk of choice
2 teaspoons sorghum syrup or
   1 teaspoon dark brown sugar
⅛ teaspoon vanilla extract

In a small bowl, mix together the turmeric, cardamom, cocoa, ginger, cloves, and allspice.

In a small saucepan over medium heat, warm the milk until heated through, 3 to 4 minutes. Stir the syrup and vanilla into the milk until completely dissolved. Sprinkle the spice powder blend into the milk mixture and reduce the heat to medium-low. Cook and stir the spiced milk for 2 to 3 minutes. Pour the hot beverage into your favorite mug or cup, using a strainer if you like.

Note: Spike it up with a jigger of rum or bourbon, for a little extra boozy warmth.

Bloody Sweet Hottie Cocktail

When my handcrafted sauces won the Flavor of Georgia competition, I was in hog heaven: I found out that the executive chef at one of Manhattan's poshest hotels loved my winning sauce and wanted to incorporate it into their Five-Diamond menu; I received a special invitation to Georgia's exclusive Sea Island Resort to be a keynote presenter and to host their signature Sea-to-Table Banquet and Weekend Event, and I also conducted workshops for their toque-blanche chefs, who left me awestruck by their culinary creativity; and I fashioned a nouveau drink after my dad's Bloody Sweet Hottie Cocktail for the oceanside reception: my award-winning sweet chili peach sauce. Here's to Fernand Petiot, the bartender at the famous St. Regis New York, who is credited for creating the original Bloody Mary in 1934. Cheers!

Serves 1

1 cup ice
1 jigger (1.5 ounces) vodka
½ cup tomato-vegetable juice
¼ cup Homemade Sweet Chili Peach Dressing (page 161)
½ teaspoon Worcestershire sauce
1 teaspoon salt
¼ teaspoon white pepper
1 fennel or celery stalk

In a cocktail mixing cup, combine the ice, vodka, tomato juice, sweet chili dressing, and Worcestershire sauce. On a small, flat plate, mix together the salt and white pepper. Moisten the rim of a glass with a wet cloth, then dip it into the salt-pepper blend to salt the rim.

Cover and shake the mixing cup well. Strain into the glass. Serve with a stalk of fennel.

Hibiscus-Pomegranate Green Tea

For me, pomegranate tea is a perennial mood-lifter, perhaps because Mother Nature blessed it with one of the most beautiful colors on Earth. When made in the summertime and served in a repurposed pickling jar packed with crushed ice, the cheery little pomegranate seeds look like Christmas ornaments floating around in the North Pole snow, creating the perfect imagery for a sweltering Georgia afternoon.

To make iced tea, cut off the strings and tags of the hibiscus tea bag and the green tea bag and place them in a large spouted carafe or glass measuring cup. Add the hot water, cover with a silicone cover or plate, and steep for 6 minutes. Remove the tea bags and add the amber rock sugar. Whisk until completely dissolved. Add the cane sugar (if using). The mixture should be twice as sweet as the desired finished taste.

Pour half of the tea into each of 2 mason jars or beverage glasses. Add half of the pomegranate juice to each glass, then add 1 tablespoon of pomegranate seeds to each glass (if using). Fill with crushed ice. For a pretty presentation, stir to blend the fruits and ice. Garnish with lemon.

Makes 2 servings

1 hibiscus tea bag or
  1 dried hibiscus flower
1 green tea bag
1 cup hot water
2 tablespoons amber rock sugar
2 teaspoons cane
  sugar (optional)
Juice of 1 pomegranate
  (about ½ cup)
2 tablespoons fresh
  pomegranate seeds
  (optional)
Crushed ice, for serving
2 lemon slices, for garnishing

Note: For a hot tea version, pour half of the tea concentrate into each of 2 microwaveable glass mugs. Add half of the pomegranate juice to each glass. Microwave for 30 seconds at a time until the desired temperature is reached. For a pretty presentation, spoon 1 tablespoon of fresh pomegranate seeds into each serving. Garnish with lemon.

Peachy-Plum Wine Sangria

A few female small-business owners and I planned a get-together recently, and one of our fellow entrepreneurs offered to host the meetup at her CEO pad in Buckhead. The sangria I created with one apple and one peach paired perfectly with tapas and conversations about work-life balance. Nothing says "sangria" like drunken fruit. And nothing says "plum perfect" like apples and peaches that have absorbed a bottle of plum wine, now a staple on my shopping list whenever I visit the iconic Tower Liquors on Buford Highway, where a growing diverse demographic is reflected in their selection of plum wines—with or without plums in it. For a Southern twist, try using a dry scuppernong wine in place of the white wine.

Serves 6

1 lime, thinly sliced in whole rounds
1 lemon, thinly sliced in whole rounds
1 cup diced apple
1 peach, thinly sliced
1 cup plum wine
¼ cup brandy
1 (750 ml) bottle white wine
Ice cubes
Unsweetened soda water, plain or lime- or lemon-flavored (optional)

In a large pitcher, combine the lime, lemon, apple, peach, plum wine, and brandy. Using a long wooden spoon, gently crush and muddle everything together for about 1 minute. Add the white wine and combine the fruit mixture and liquid. Add ice to the pitcher and serve in wineglasses.

For a light, sparkling touch, add a splash of soda water and more ice to each glass.

Dad's Classic Sweet Iced Tea

People used to walk across the mall and stand in line for a "large sweet tea" from our restaurant. It was my dad's idea to pair egg rolls with his signature iced tea, freshly brewed in-house from premium loose black tea, then sweetened and brought to another level with a generous infusion of fresh-squeezed Georgia lemons. Make it your own, with more or less sugar and lemon.

Serves 6

2 large ripe lemons

¼ cup loose English breakfast tea

1 Ten Ren high mountain oolong tea bag

2 cups boiling water

1 cup amber rock sugar

Ice cubes, for serving

Cold filtered water, for serving

Boil a kettle of water. In contrast to the delicate leaves of Taiwanese oolong tea, which are steeped off the boil, English tea is a rich, bold black tea, requiring a full boil for proper steeping. That is a professional definition. For household preparation, there is no discernible difference off-boil or full-boil as long as the water temperature does not fall below 190°F when pouring over the tea leaves.

While the water is heating, prepare the lemons. Cut lemon in half lengthwise, then cut each half into 3 wedges, resulting in 6 total lemon wedges, to be used for flavoring the sweet tea concentrate upon serving. (Some folks may not want lemon, so we always add it to serving glasses rather than to the pitcher).

Cut the second lemon in half lengthwise. Cut a slit along the middle pith line, but don't cut through the peel. Turn the lemon half over so the flesh is facing down. Cut off the ends. Slice the remainder of the lemon half into three equal pieces. Set aside for garnishing.

To make a full-bodied freshly brewed tea concentrate, you will need 2 (32-ounce) mason jars or 2 (4-cup) glass measuring cups. Put the English breakfast tea in 1 jar. Cut the tag and string off the oolong tea bag and drop it in with the loose tea. Pour in the boiling water, cover with a silicone cover or plate, and steep for 4 to 7 minutes. Every 30-second interval will make a difference in the strength of the brewed tea, so at the 4-minute mark, test every half a minute or so and determine the optimal brewing time to taste (4 minutes is considered a light brew for English tea, which is known for its robustness, while 7 minutes might be too bitter for some palates).

continued

Once the tea finishes steeping, strain the liquid into the second glass jar. Add the amber rock sugar to the strained tea. Whisk or stir until completely dissolved. The tea should be dark brown and taste twice as sweet and strong as the desired finished taste.

To serve right away, pour ½ cup of the sweetened tea concentrate into each serving glass. Add the juice of 1 lemon wedge, if desired. Fill the glass with ice. Top off with filtered water (to avoid any chlorine taste). Stir briefly to mix. Garnish by clipping the slit lemon onto the rim of each glass.

To chill and serve later, pour ½ cup of the sweetened tea concentrate per serving into a pitcher. Refrigerate until ready to serve. Prepare the lemons, then follow the above instructions for serving in glasses.

Notes: After the tea leaves and tea bag are steeped, they are no longer needed. To make extra tea, I usually add 1 cup of hot water to the leftover tea leaves and bag and steep for another 3 to 5 minutes. Steeping too long will cause bitterness. If the tea ends up bitter, try adding a dash of baking soda while it is still warm so the soda can fully dissolve before chilling. Strain and discard the used leaves and tea bag. Store this batch separately—do not add it to the first steep.

English breakfast tea is ideal, but any full-bodied black or red loose tea can be substituted. Tea bags can be used (1 tea bag per teaspoon of loose tea), although the result will not be as optimal as the distinct aromatic beverage that is rendered from fresh loose tea. Adding 1 or 2 additional high mountain oolong tea bags will add flavor (always cut off the strings and labels). Remove the bags after 4 minutes.

In a pinch, use 2 tablespoons of organic turbinado sugar per serving.

Resource Guide

These are some of the long-kept secrets that infuse Asian flavors, plus Southernness, into the recipes in this cookbook—shared here, for the first time: an alphabetized list of specialty ingredients, where to find them, how I source them, why I choose to use them. Your support and patronage of local growers, mom-and-pop producers, and diverse suppliers will make a positive difference—not only in quality and taste, but also in the "meaningfulness" of each dish. Your choices create a ripple effect, up and down the supply chain.

Also showcased are some nonprofits doing amazing work to improve underserved communities from which I drew inspiration. I will be donating a portion of my sales proceeds from this book to organizations such as these, as well as female- and minority-owned businesses in Georgia and resource networks for women. I hope you'll join me in thanking them by supporting their good causes.

APPLEWOOD SMOKED BACON. Mildly sweet and smoky bacon smoked with applewood chips, the second most popular wood used after hickory. Century-old bacon legacy, now third generation. Tastes great in Oven-Baked Country Bacon & Collard Egg Rolls (page 24). WrightBrand.com (use their online locator to find a local store).

AVOCADO OIL is usually marketed with one or more labels, including unrefined, refined, raw, virgin, and cold-pressed. Use 1:1 as a substitute for any vegetable oil. Adds a clean, light flavor in Beyond Fried Rice with Free-Range Eggs (page 44).

BETTER THAN BOUILLON BEEF (soup base). Organic roasted beef soup based. Generally available at supermarkets. Perfect for Night Market Cracked Peppercorn Steak Gravy (page 155). BetterThanBouillon.com

BLACK SESAME POWDER for Black Sesame & Almond Mini Croissants (page 170). Xiangyuan Roasted Black Sesame Powder (Taiwan) and other brands. Taiwan is known for its stringent government protocols. Look for products with U.S. distributors and no additives and no artificial colors or flavors. SayWeee.com

Dip. Drizzle. Toss. Stir fry. My natural-fusion sauces are recipients of the prestigious sofi Award and Flavor of Georgia winners. Time to create more sauce babies!

BLACK SHORT-GRAIN RICE. I call it revolutionary rice. Since 2008, Lotus Foods' More Crop Per Drop program has partnered with small-scale farmers worldwide to double and even triple their yields using up to 50 percent less water. Rainbow Black Rice Salad (page 38) features this nutritious, nutty, noir "Forbidden Rice." LotusFoods.com

BLACK SILKIE CHICKEN OR BLACK SILKIE BANTAM. One of the oldest chicken breeds. Contains one-third fewer calories and half the fat of regular chicken. To buy American, opt for California-raised Grimaud Farms Silkie Black Chicken, frozen (5000+ sold per year). Or Wingtat Silkie Black Chicken, "La Soyeuse Poulet," which is homegrown in Canada. Almost always sold with head and feet intact. See Whole Silkie Black Chicken Soup (page 121). SayWeee.com or GlobalHearth.com

BLACK "STICKY" GLUTINOUS RICE, sometimes labeled "sweet Black Thai rice" is featured in Natalie's Signature Purple Snushi Rolls (page 28). GlobalHearth.com or Nuts.com

BOUILLON (meatless). Dark horse founder and restaurateur Greg uses organic ingredients to create umami flavors without sugars and preservatives. If you can afford to support sustainable production and packaging, consider the extra cost as an investment to benefit your health and the planet. I like their umami bouillon for Mom's Unfried Red Rice with Berries (page 46). darkhorseorganic.com

CAMELLIA OIL is a tea seed oil packed with polyphenols, vitamin E, and antioxidant properties and packing more omega-3s than olive oil. It is native to Hunan province. A perfect, healthful pairing with Turmeric Steamed Brown Rice (page 45).

CHILE PEPPERS. When shopping for chile peppers, such as in Hot Hot Hunan Fresh Chile Sambal (page 159), support local farmers' markets and international grocers, and look to Michael and Patty of Chili Pepper Madness to learn about chili pepper varieties. ChiliPepperMadness.com

CHILI CRUNCH is key to my Creamy Chili Crisp Aioli (page 156). Enjoy ready-made from Lao Gan Ma at Asian international super-markets, made by local chefs and purveyors or at GlobalHearth.com.

CHILI SAUCE, HOT (CHINESE, TAIWANESE, KOREAN). Since 1950, Ming Teh (Taiwan) Broadbean Paste with Chilies (heat level is medium) has sat right next to soy sauce. Use it in Japchae-Inspired Glass Noodles with Swiss Chard (page 107).

DASHI POWDER. Dashi generally refers to a powdered soup base that imparts an umami taste. Hondashi is a popular Japanese brand (Hondashi is to dashi powder as Crisco is to shortening), while *dashi no moto* is a blanket term. Dark Horse Umami Powder is a stellar stand-in. Drunken Ginger All-Purpose Asian-y Minced Pork Filling (page 135) is one of a gazillion uses for this pan-Asian pantry staple. Try kayanoya.com for fancy-shmancy, or GlobalHearth.com or your local Asian grocer.

FISH SAUCE. MegaChef Fish Sauce contains no artificial flavors colors, no preservatives, and is gluten-free. Magical in Thai Memories Macadamia Nut Dressing & Toss Sauce (page 154). www.megachefsauce.com.

FRIED WONTON STRIPS as a topping in Broccoli & Basmati Rice Casserole (page 50) and salads. Fry up your own using wonton or dumpling wrappers or buy at Target, Walmart, or Whole Foods.

GINGER ROOT. Like turmeric, ginger is technically a rhizome that boasts strong medicinal benefits. Fresh, even fresh-frozen is far superior over ground ginger or in a jar. Select pieces that are firm and have shiny, taut skin, not desiccated. Store fresh-frozen whole ginger in a sealed pouch. Use in my Meal-in-a-Bowl Kimchi Veggie Fried Rice (page 48). Available fresh in most grocery stores.

GOCHUCHANG KOREAN HOT SAUCE. O'Food Medium Hot Gochujang sauce is kosher, vegan, and contains no corn syrup. Traditional Korean recipe using brown rice, fermented soybeans, and red chile peppers. Perfect in Auspicious Fish: Banquet-Style Whole Pompano (page 142). Sayweee.com or GlobalHearth.com

HARISSA SEASONING (POWDER) in Harissa-Spiced Edamame Pods (page 96) is a traditional North African blend of select chiles, cumin, garlic, mint, and more. Frontier Cooperative, member-owned since 1976, carries organic, kosher, nonirradiated, sustainably grown ingredients. Frontiercoop.com

HOISIN SAUCE, a thick, sweet, and salty sauce of soybeans, fennel, red chile peppers, and garlic often used in Cantonese dishes, and featured in my Mu Shu Wood Ear Burritos (page 79). The translation of "hoisin" is seafood, but it is primarily used in dark, savory meat dishes, rather than for seafood. Based in Hong Kong, the venerable Lee Kum Kee brand has made hoisin since 1888. Readily available in most supermarkets.

HONEY, SOURWOOD. Bold and complex sourwood honey for the deliciously simple pairing in Moon over Wasabi: 1-Minute Avocado Scoop & Dip (page 114) originates mostly in the southern Appalachian regions of North Carolina, Tennessee, and Georgia. Sourwood has a buttery, caramel flavor and is one of the most sought-after kinds of honey in the world. GlobalHearth.com or directly from local beekeepers and honey farmers.

KALE, DINOSAUR. Also known as Lacinato or Tuscan kale, dinosaur kale is darker green and more tender than curly kale, making it perfect for Dinosaur Kale & Asian Pear Salad (page 108). Support local growers at your farmers' market or grocery store.

KEWPIE JAPANESE-STYLE MAYONNAISE uses only egg yolks for a rich, slightly sweet taste. Perfect for Creamy Chili Crisp Aioli (page 156) and Yellow & Green Panko Squash Fries (page 73). Support your local Asian and international supermarket or GlobalHearth.com.

LAUREL SESAME SWEET RICE BALLS ("tang yuan"). Find these in the frozen food section of some markets. They come in several filling flavors, but for Sweet Rice Balls & Bols with Pear (page 176), use sweet black sesame. For space-saving storage, remove the balls, recycle the tray, and put the balls back in the bag. SayWeee.com

LYCHEE FRUIT. For Lychee Fruit Cocktail with Almond Gelatin (page 172), I use Asian Best Lychee in Syrup or Shirakiku Lychee Seedless Whole Can. When in season, grab the fresh fruit (grown in Florida and California) for a special treat. Just remove the shell and seed.

MATCHA GREEN TEA POWDER. Shade-grown, finely milled green tea featured in Gotcha Matcha Ice Cream Pie (page 169) and Black Sesame Cupcakes with Matcha Frosting (page 178) from Ten Ren Tea Company, founded in Taiwan in 1953. TenRen.com

MIRIN (HON MIRIN). Japanese sweet rice cooking wine. Hon mirin means "real" mirin made from only three ingredients: glutinous rice, shochu (a distilled liquor), and koji (rice malt), the umami booster in miso, soy sauce, and sake. It's the magic in Sesame Sammie Spread & Veggie Dip (page 162). Think of hon mirin as 100% maple syrup and aji mirin ("taste-alike mirin") as mass-produced maple-flavored syrup. Aji mirin, made with water, corn syrup, alcohol, rice, and salt, is more widely available. TheJapanStore.us

MUNG BEAN NOODLES, glass, or cellophane noodles are flavorless, and in Fried Chicken Spring Rolls with Honey (page 20) and Chayote & Georgia White Shrimp Egg Rolls (page 22), these tender numbers help absorb the flavors of sauces, herbs, and other aromatics. Or they can feature as a main dish in Japchae-Inspired Glass Noodles with Swiss Chard (page 107). The threads are gelatinous and sometimes appear translucent when cooked.

MUSHROOMS, SHIITAKE. Support sustainable mushroom farmers. Ellijay Mushrooms started on land in the North Georgia mountains shared with Buddhist monks. No wonder, in Sake-Shiitake Mushroom Bake (page 78), their shiitake mushrooms and gorgeous "bouquets" of oyster mushrooms taste out of this world. Support EllijayMushrooms.com or your local mushroom farmers.

MUSHROOMS, SHIMEJI. Shimeji mushrooms come in brown or white. Just cut off the bottoms, and rinse. They're tender, so further chopping is optional, for visual presentation, as in Meal-in-a-Bowl Kimchi Veggie Fried Rice (page 48). SayWeee.com or your local mushroom farmers

OLIVE OIL. If possible, support local produce. Otherwise support your local green packager. Mine is Georgia Olive Farms, whose homegrown olives from their groves in Lakeland, Georgia, are pressed within 24 hours. To die for in my Rebel Asian Pesto (page 157). Try different varieties for subtle overtones in Sesame Sammie Spread & Veggie Dip (page 162). GeorgiaOlivefarms.com or GlobalHearth.com

PICKLED GINGER or "gari" is the perfect palate cleanser and companion to Natalie's Signature Purple Snushi Rolls (page 28), and a blob of pickled ginger always takes the corner spot on my charcuterie boards! The Ginger People Organic Pickled Sushi Ginger is USDA Organic with no artificial coloring. GingerPeople.com

RICE VERMICELLI NOODLES are a thin form of rice noodles similar to angel hair pasta. Use them in Smoked Salmon Summer Rolls (page 17).

RICE VINEGAR, DARK OR CHINESE BLACK VINEGAR. Mellow, complex flavor, and relatively light acidity. Balsamic vinegar is a handy substitute, although it's made from grapes and tends to be a bit sweeter. Worcestershire sauce, such as suggested in I-Lava-You Island Chunky BBQ Sauce with Pineapple & Coconut Sugar (page 160), is also an option, though spicier. SayWeee.com or GlobalHearth.com

RICE WINE, Taiwanese. In Asian cooking, rice wine is used like cooking sherry. The essence of sweet rice elevates all the flavor-ful elements of my I-Lava-You Island Chunky BBQ Sauce with Pineapple & Coconut Sugar (page 160). If you're lucky enough to get your hands on some, Taiwan's Hong Biou ("Red Label") MiJiu is the top-of-the-line rice wine. SayWeee.com or GlobalHearth.com

SAUSAGE, all kinds. Pine Street Market's country sausage (no antibiotics, no hormones) for Seedy Pigs in a Blanket with Wasabi Mustard (page 89), their Andouille sausage or Carroll's smoked link sausage for Himalayan Red Rice & Beans (page 54), and their pork chops for Grandma's Teriyaki Pork Chops (page 131). Support your local butcher, PineStreetMarket.com, or CarrollsSausage.com.

SESAME OIL. Kadoya 100% Pure (Roasted) Sesame Oil, from Japan. Roasted (or toasted) sesame oil is a game-changer in Kawaii Calamari Twice-Fried Gyoza Fritters (page 27). Try adding a few drops as a nutty finisher to any soup (contrastingly, plain sesame oil is neutral and used for cooking). Go to SayWeee.com, your neigh-borhood Japanese grocer, or a local international supermarket.

SHAOXING RICE WINE. An amber-colored rice wine made from fermented rice and wheat (not gluten-free), which imparts a mildly sweet hint of sake. For cooking, the cheaper version (with salt) works fine. But for drinking warmed, usually over a dried sour plum and served in a shot glass, splurge for the premium Taiwanese kind. Differs from clear rice wine. SayWee.com or GlobalHearth.com

SHICHIMI TOGARASHI. The classic, somewhat nutty, umami-spicy, bit-salty-bit-tangy, Japanese 7-spice blend that inspired my Seven-Spice Lemon Garlic Georgia Shrimp (page 139) and is now surging in popularity across the culinary spectrum. SpiceJungle.com or GlobalHearth.com

SORGHUM SYRUP in the Golden Milk & Sorghum Hot Toddy (page 193) adds a deep, buttery sweetness and is rich in nutri-ents like manganese, vitamin B-6, magnesium, and potassium. Produced mainly in the "Sorghum Belt" of the Southern Great

Plains like Kentucky and Oklahoma, it's worth the special buy. MuddyPondSorghum.com, Etsy.com, or GlobalHearth.com

SOUTHERN SECRET MUSCADINE MOONSHINE in the Night Market Cracked Peppercorn Steak Gravy (page 155) is hand-crafted in small batches with no additives at Swamp Fox Distilling Company. SwampFoxDistillingco.com

SOY SAUCE, NATURALLY BREWED. Kimlan Soy Sauce Paste (thick), Kimlan Job's Tears, Grade-A Light Soy Sauce. My Homemade Soy-Ginger Sauce (page 164) taps the complexity of this famous soy sauce brand, made in Taiwan since 1936. Saywee.com

SPRING ROLL RICE PAPER WRAPPERS, round, Vietnamese-style for Smoked Salmon Summer Rolls (page 17). Support your local Asian or international grocer or a woman-owned business, GlobalHearth.com.

SUSHI RICE. Medium grain Japanese rice that's perfect for making Turkey Burger Sliders on Grilled Rice Buns (page 124). Support your local international grocer or USA growers Lundberg Family Farms Organic Sushi Rice, California rice available at Whole Foods or Walmart. Try American Sushi Rice at GlobalHearth.com and Lotus Foods' certified organic Jade Pearl Rice, a pesticide-free sushi rice infused with wild crafted bamboo extract. LotusFoods.com

SWEET POTATO STARCH, GRAINY (or "thick" although mis-translated). Imperial Taste Thick Sweet Potato Starch works great for Flying Chicken Roasted BBQ Wingettes (page 94). SayWee.com

TEMPEH. Available at most supermarkets in the natural food section or, to switch up Meal-in-a-Bowl Kimchi Veggie Fried Rice (page 48) try hempeh—soy-free, gluten-free, hemp-fortified tempeh, made with raw hemp seeds and organic legumes like black beans and peanuts, from family-owned SmilingHaraTempeh.com.

TURMERIC, like ginger root, is technically a rhizome with a mild orange and ginger fragrance highlighted in Curried Coconut-Cauliflower Fried "Rice" (page 53) and Turmeric Steamed Brown Rice (page 45). With numerous medicinal and anti-inflammatory healing properties, including soothing upset tummies, Golden Milk & Sorghum Hot Toddy (page 193) or turmeric latte, is the key. Sold fresh in many Asian international grocery stores or seasonally at farmers' markets. Store fresh turmeric in the freezer.

VEGETARIAN MUSHROOM OYSTER SAUCE. Wan Ja Shan is Taiwan's most famous producer of premium soy sauces. Made from a proprietary blend of mushrooms, soybeans, wheat, salt, and sugar to impart a rich umami flavor, their Vegetarian Mushroom Oyster Sauce gives perfect balance for Meal-in-a-Bowl Kimchi Veggie Fried Rice (page 48). Vegan, non-GMO, no MSG, 100 percent naturally brewed, no artificial coloring. GlobalHearth.com

VINDALOO CURRY SPICE PASTE. Patak's Vindaloo Curry Spice Paste (paprika, red pepper, turmeric, cumin) is MSG-free and a versatile base for dishes like my Vindaloo-Inspired Ratatouille Ziti (page 68). Explore your local Indian grocer, Asian supermarket, or PatakUSA.com.

WASABI, AMERICAN-STYLE horseradish powder or paste that adds the potent, peppery edge to Wasabi Deviled Eggs (page 91) is readily available in most supermarkets and Japanese grocers.

YUCA (OR CASSAVA) in Home Alone Garlicky Cilantro Yuca (page 92) is conveniently available pre-peeled and frozen in most international or Hispanic supermarkets. Because the peels and leaves are toxic, yuca should never be eaten raw. SayWee.com

Draped by Atlanta's city skyline, this invitational rooftop culinary presentation for the Global Commerce Council received accolades for cross-cultural business insights, and nifty stir-frying tips.

SUPPORT OUR COMMUNITY ALLIES in the movement for civil and human rights; sustainability; and clean, good, fair food:

- Asian Americans Advancing Justice (www.advancingjustice-aajc.org)

- Asian American Advocacy Fund (www.asianamericanadvocacyfund.org)

- Captain Planet Foundation (captainplanetfoundation.org)

- Center for Pan-Asian Community Services (cpacs.org)

- Charles H. Bassett Youth Foundation (www.facebook.com/FriendsofCHBYouthFoundation)

- CivilEats.com (civileats.com)

- Community Farmers Markets (cfmatl.org)

- Divas With a Cause (divaswithacause.org)

- Georgia Organics (www.georgiaorganics.org)

- Giving Kitchen (thegivingkitchen.org)

- Global Growers (globalgrowers.org)

- Global Hearth (globalhearth.com)

- Hostel in the Forest (www.foresthostel.com)

- Leadership Atlanta (leadershipatlanta.org)

- Les Dames d'Escoffier International (ldei.org)

- Let's Talk Womxn (letstalkwomxn.com)

- Metro Atlanta Cycling Club (maccattack.com)

- The National Center for Civil and Human Rights (civilandhumanrights.org)

- No Kid Hungry (www.nokidhungry.org)

- Project Drawdown (drawdown.org)

- ReFED (reducing food waste) (refed.org)

- Slow Food Movement (www.slowfood.com)

- Stop AAPI Hate (data-based tracking) (stopaapihate.org)

Acknowledgments

To **the women of Atlanta**, whose resounding inspiration engendered the concept of a food-for-thought cookbook: **Dr. Bernice King** (The Martin Luther King, Jr. Center for Nonviolent Social Change), grounded and principled visionary, for enlightening me on this "long march" to replace anger with action, and for advocating the ideals of peace and nonviolence of your mother without getting lost in the legacy and limelight. Eco-warrior **Laura Turner Seydel** and the Captain Planet Foundation, been a fan since the time I introduced your daughter L.E. at Taste of Atlanta, the female-founded festival that showcases our hometown culinary landscape (kudos, **Dale DeSena**). Executive Chef **Holly Chute**, for introducing my sauces to Georgia's First Family—it's an honor to grace the Governor's Mansion menu. **Gail Evans**, comrade in the fight for gender equality in corporate America and revered author of *Play Like a Man, Win Like a Woman*—I thought of you when **Julia Chan** (now editor in chief at The 19th) featured me in CNN's *Start Small Think Big*. We are moving the needle, but there's still a lot of Tara-on-Techwood ground to cover.

Judith Winfrey, farmer and entrepreneur, who would become my wise and gracious mentor at Les Dames d'Escoffier International (LDEI) and **Julie Shaffer** (Slow Food International) for being there when my business was barely off the ground. Chefs and fellow authors, **Jennifer Booker and Deborah VanTrece**, for transforming the industry landscape by infusing "global local" expertise (a reminder of who isn't seated at the table), and for never being "too busy" to offer advice and support for newbies; and, fellow Dames on the LDEI **National Diversity Task Force** who broadened my insights outside the Southern region. The Cook's Warehouse founder turned SVP at IMC (wow) and fellow female entrepreneur, **Mary Moore**, for our launch of Atlanta's first hands-on Asian cooking class, I am a grateful beneficiary of your vision, plus your mesmerizing retail wonderland gave me a gajillion "excuses to cook." **Marion Nestle**, our conversations after the Fancy Food

Top: Bernice King and Natalie at a Beloved Community Talks event.

Bottom: Gail Evans and Natalie at a Leadership Atlanta women's retreat.

Show in NYC about food politics led to my certification as a health educator and my election to public office.

Master gardener **Robin Pollack** and husband **Marc Pollack**, author of *Chez Marc's Quarantine Cookbook* benefitting the **Gateway Center**, ever since we met on my **Southern Foodways Alliance** food tour, just want to let you know how much my mom and I have enjoyed your company (and figs from your famous "yard") over the years, so thank you for the rarity of your organic friendship, so pure and simple, for it is something cooked up by the heavens that can't be recipe'd. **Kim Bui Barnett**, award-winning producer and journalist whose family pioneered Atlanta's Vietnamese media scene. Ovations for being lifelong Champions for Change! Former national news anchor and Emperor of Japan Award recipient **Sachi Koto**, the first Japanese on-air talent in the Southeast and the first Asian on-air talent in Atlanta, kudos for cracking through the bamboo ceiling. And love to **Margie and Gus Levy**, my parents' Jewish host family. You opened your home and hearts in 1960s Houston to a young Rice University grad student named Edward, who had traveled from a tiny island nation on the far side of the Pacific, and his beloved Margaret, who would become my mother.

To my fellow **Harvard Kennedy School alumni**—past, present, and future—often feeling like the last of the true believers, daring to create a more perfect union through democratic ideals, fair and just government, and public service. In 1996, my policy paper on how a diversity hiring initiative at the **New England Aquarium** "backfired" was selected for publication. This led to my role as Associate Director at the The National Conference for Community and Justice. After five years, I left the nonprofit to drive change in the corporate world. I am grateful for the unique journey of job rejections that ensued, but even more thankful to that one female hiring manager who compassionately cued me in: "If you're a girl, Ivy League means you're too expensive or overqualified." I promptly deleted Harvard from my resume. It worked. I joined a Fortune 100 giant in the world of financial services and acquired priceless work experience, like being constantly instructed, "one sugar, no cream" (girls get the coffee, even if they're VPs). This left me starkly aware of gender bias in the C-suite. But the proof is now in the pudding: A major data-based analysis by Morgan Stanley (2022) shows that

Natalie with Mom (Margaret) and Dad (Edward) on graduation day at Harvard Kennedy School.

factoring in boardroom diversity can, indeed, improve yields on large-cap equity stock selection. So high-five, **Harvard Alumni for Global Women's Empowerment**, for our relentless advocacy that bringing women to the table benefits the bottom line. Here's to vindication, twenty years in the making, worthy of uncorking a bottle of '96 Chateau Margaux.

To **James Montoya**, former dean of Vassar College, where the writings of Audre Lorde in Women's Studies changed my philosophy of life, and the late **Mary Gesek** (Alumni Association)—whose nudging turned my "gut feelings" into action and resulted in Vassar's first-ever multicultural dialogues on race and spawned the Asian Pacific Alumni of Vassar College (APAVC)—though often lumped together by ethnic stereotyping, each of our stories is as bespoke as they are awesome. Fellow alum, polyglot, and *migliore amico* **Rob D'Emilio**, in defiance of 17th-century physicians who diagnosed nostalgia as a mental affliction, I love wallowing in the memories of our *famiglia* trip to Deliceto, Italy, the long splintery table overlooking the fields, freshly picked *fiori di zucca,* and, ooh, that warm handful of *knotted mozzarella di bufala* in the wee hours of morning, after strolling down cobblestone streets lined with flower boxes for your cousin's provincial wedding serenata. Let's do it again.

Susan Musinsky (Social Innovation Forum), prescient co-conspirator at the **National Conference for Community and Justice (NCCJ),** for having my back as we busted stereotyping in schools, compelled CEOs to redress systemic inequities, and redefined the tenets of leadership development. Beau, NCCJ ally, penultimate servant-leader, and exemplar of courage, integrity, and selflessness—I am profoundly humbled to take part in the legacy you're building as an agent of change; on behalf of the young minds whose worldview will be augmented by **Bassett Youth Foundation** scholarships, thank you, from sea to shining sea (New York and Alaska). **Kevin So**, NCCJ friend and groundbreaking musician-singer-songwriter, your can-do spirit is a constant reminder that staying true to oneself will triumph over critics and naysayers. **Nate Olson**, optics, tech, and branding expert, you believed in me before I did and set up my first online shop—forever indebted, my talented friend. **Bailey Barash**, filmmaker and videographer, in gratitude for your support in the early days and for persuading me to document my cherished Taiwan-to-Smyrna family stories.

Top: Beau Bassett, Natalie, and Mom (Margaret) at Denali National Park in Alaska.

Bottom: Natalie, Kevin So, and Monk, the singing dog.

As the only Asian American appointee on the **Governor's Health Task Force (Community Outreach)**, I applaud those who stepped up to protect the underrepresented. We came together for a worthy cause under dire circumstances. **Victoria Huynh** (Center for Pan-Asian Community Services), for your grassroots efforts to increase accessibility to community services, and **Rohini Dey**, for founding **Let's Talk Womxn** amidst a global pandemic, you exemplified the phrase "out of crisis comes opportunity" (the Mandarin word for "crisis" is a portmanteau coined from "danger" and "opportunity"); LTW's fast-growing network of business resources and collaborative energy benefited me and dozens of female founders and local proprietors. Shout out to the cheerful "Popsicle cartrepreneurs" at **King of Pops** and owner **Nick Carse**, as much as I love Popsicles, I was over the moon when a serendipitous do-si-do during the pandemic made you my sauce distributor and business partner.

Audra D. Luke, climate activist-global humanitarian-youth impactor with a JD and author of *From Powerless to Empowered*, our "walk talks" are not merely dialogues on nature, Caribbean food, and B-52s lyrics syncopated with jolts of laughter, they are oxygen for my soul. And "six degrees of **Atiba Mbiwan** and **Bruce Morton**," you both had me at "hi," yet still show up on the hottest—and coldest—days at the farmers' market, stoke fundraisers with your connections, and never fail to brighten my day. To **Gene**, **Charles**, and **Parks,**your scholarship pageant exudes positivity and inclusiveness throughout the community. **My sister, Leigh**, who was the first Asian-American to win a local Miss America Preliminary, has continued to carry forward the power of volunteerism by supporting Georgia's Disabled American Veterans, Fishing for Freedom, and Dress for Success. **Sheri Mann Stewart**, mother, producer, writer, and activist, proving we can do it all and still be there for each other; how much it meant that you were a regular at my Joy Potluck gatherings where women, food, and stories came together.

My treasured **Georgia Grown** family, like **Ross Harding** (Verdant Kitchen), thanks heaps, mate, and **Keith** and **Nikki Schroeder** for invaluable advice and educating me "from scratch" about artisan craft foods. **Matthew Kulinski** (Department of Agriculture) and the Georgia Grown program staff—where would the Peach (and pecan) State be without y'all? And my cohort of **Buford Highway** businesses and restaurants, many immigrant-owned, situated

Leigh Keng, Gene Phillips, Natalie, and Mom (Margaret) at the 1980 Miss Georgia Pageant.

in a corridor that was historically overlooked for redevelopment funding—who enthusiastically partnered with me as a "food tour guide" on a mission to demystify ethnic products and spotlight local purveyors. Pioneer **Harold Shinn** (Buford Highway Farmers Market) for launching the first series of Asian cooking classes with me in an international supermarket; **Ben Vo** (City Farmers Markets) host-magnifique to my food tour groups; and **Cam Vuong** (Canton House) applauded host of our annual Lunar New Year Cultural Dinner and Banquet since 2009, who came to America as a teenager with only $20 and the shirt on his back but now beams with pride that his children are university graduates.

Janice Shay (Pinafore Press), agent, book packager, and advocate, your name is a homophone for "thank you" in Mandarin, so *shay-shay* for being my quarterback extraordinaire. You are the quintessential "steel magnolia" with a genius for balancing cheer-leading, play calls, and project management with utmost Southern grace. Food stylist, **Angela Hinkel**, there are angels, and there are OMG angels. That's you. I know you are bound for the bigger and better, but I hope you will always remember our shared beginning, for had our career trajectories not pivoted in synchrony, I would have missed the delightful honor of working with you; thank you for exemplifying the ultimate calm-n-cool professionalism as you worked your magic in creating order from chaos. **Michelle Branson** and the Gibbs Smith team, for allowing this long-simmering vision of mine to burgeon into a salient Asian-American-Southern motif for the pondering mind and the curious palate. And Atlanta photographer **Deborah Whitlaw Llewellyn**, bless your incredible eye for elevating simple to elegant, for rendering confidence without hubris, and for capturing the unorthodox mindset that this project represents: a celebration of commonalities in an ever-diverse culinary zeitgeist.

Bushels of thanks to my devoted sauce fans and hometown supporters, including my old classmates and Mom's past students. And, to the umpteen interns and volunteers who helped when this project was a charity event, a food show booth, a farmers' market stand, a garden-to-wok demo at the botanical gardens, a technical workshop for classically trained "western" chefs, an international grocery and restaurants tour, a Happy Anniversary dumpling-making soirée, a cross-cultural professional development experience

Top: Coach Ron Jackson congratulates Natalie, Ultimate Tennis doubles champion.

Bottom: Community leaders and cycling buddies, David Southerland and Atiba Mbiwan, stay in shape while solving global problems.

for corporate exec teams and law firms around Metro-Atlanta and beyond. Hugs to teen fan **Amelia Vinson** (and teacher-mom Jacqueline), thank you for loving my sauces and for always gifting them to your teachers. My Sweet Hottie and Wild Wild East have been "dipped" in public school cafeterias serving 180,000 students! I've watched you "grow up" as we walked years of "funky and eclectic" Inman Park Festival parades together, and I adore your cheerful art messages. Tennis coach **Ron Jackson**, from your lessons, I have drawn respite and nourishment when my plate is too full, gleaned insights for winning in the game of life, and learned the true meaning of "love-all." To you I owe an intimidating backhand and a hefty bowlful of grit.

Heartfelt gratitude to **David Southerland**, past president of the Atlanta Bicycle Campaign and longtime active member-organizer of the Metro Atlanta Cycling Club (MACC), for sponsoring bike rides for public school teens of all colors, from under-resourced households, around themes that promote leadership, fitness, and history. As a ride co-leader for women and beginners, I've seen many "scared" faces light up with confidence and joy. The 1,200+ rider **One Love Century** fundraisers you help organize are, hands down, the best charity bike ride in the Southeast. You joke that it's the rest-stop snacks and the post-ride Jamaican patty gatherings I come for, but you know in your heart that it's the camaraderie I savor most. In your day job as Executive Director of the **American Institute of Architects**, your unswerving efforts to foster participation by women and minority architects (NOMA), through mentoring and reducing barriers in a male-dominated profession, deserve an ovation for demonstrating the kind of organizational leadership it takes to design and build inclusive portals and gateways to opportunity.

To my **dad**, for his utter enjoyment of country music and his unforgettable baritone rendition of "Put Another Log on the Fire." Our father-daughter memories—and a pig's ear sandwich from Wyatt's—fueled me through many a late night of troubleshooting supply chain issues in a quarantine world. Finally, to my trailblazer **mom** and millions like her, here and yonder, who defiantly chisel away at glass ceilings to forge their own careers, while dutifully morphing into kitchen gladiators on nights and weekends, to preserve—and lovingly embellish—the flavors of humanity that bring everyone to the table.

Top: Young Dad (Edward).

Bottom: Young Mom (Margaret). Mom and Dad chose the names Edward and Margaret after Prince Edward and Princess Margaret.

Index

Metric Conversion Chart

Volume Measurements		Weight Measurements		Temperature Conversion	
U.S.	*Metric*	*U.S.*	*Metric*	*Fahrenheit*	*Celsius*
1 teaspoon	5 ml	½ ounce	15 g	250	120
1 tablespoon	15 ml	1 ounce	30 g	300	150
¼ cup	60 ml	3 ounces	90 g	325	160
⅓ cup	75 ml	4 ounces	115 g	350	180
½ cup	125 ml	8 ounces	225 g	375	190
⅔ cup	150 ml	12 ounces	350 g	400	200
¾ cup	175 ml	1 pound	450 g	425	220
1 cup	240 ml	2¼ pounds	1 kg	450	230

NATALIE KENG is the founder/CEO (Chief Eating Officer) of Global Hearth, a multifaceted business that leverages the power of food and culture to promote team building and diversity inclusion through its Cooking Up a Better World platform of Eat-the-World tours and Stir-Fried America presentations. Nicknamed the Chinese Southern Belle, Keng created an award-winning line of cooking sauces that feature local ingredients and harken back to old family recipes, earning her the moniker "The Sauce Maven." Before starting her own business, Keng was a Fortune 100 marketing executive, headed leadership development for national nonprofits, and served in public office. Keng received the Greater Women's Business Council's Trailblazer Award and was appointed to the governor's Health Task Force. A graduate of Vassar College, Keng holds a Master's of Public Policy from the Harvard Kennedy School. She lives in her hometown of Smyrna, Georgia.